. *World Famous* .

MISTAKES

Jesse Flowerfoot
and Esme Hawes

MAGPIE
London

Magpie Books Ltd
7 Kensington Church Court
London W8 4SP

First published in the UK 1994
Copyright © Magpie Books Ltd
Illustrations and cover pictures © Popperfoto

ISBN 1 85813 4005

Typeset by Hewer Text Composition Services, Edinburgh
Printed in Finiand by
Werner Söderström Oy

Contents

・ **chapter one** ・

OPPORTUNITY FLOPS

O pportunity Flops is mistake category 1. It is that special moment in any person's life when they are, quite suddenly, presented with a golden opportunity to achieve glory, honour and fame. And then they blow it. Everyone knows where they were when Waddle booted it over the bar. It was that once in a lifetime opportunity and he missed. He came. He saw. He cocked it up.

Charge of the Light Brigade

One of the most famous mistakes in military history was undoubtedly the Charge of the Light Brigade but very few people actually know what happened.

The British base at Balaclava was under attack from the Russian army during the Crimean War in 1854. The Russians had taken some high ground near the town, but the British had thrown them into disarray through a powerful heavy cavalry charge led by General Scarlett.

Lord Raglan, the British Commander-in-Chief, was watching the battle from the top of a nearby hill. He saw the damage that Scarlett's charge had done and wanted to follow it up with a light cavalry charge, supported by infantry. He therefore sent a message to his cavalry commander Lord Lucan, which read "Cavalry to advance and take advantage of any opportunity to recover Heights. They will be supported by the infantry, who have been ordered to advance on two fronts."

From Lucan's position in the valley below, it was not clear what the message meant. He couldn't see the place he was supposed to be attacking and decided to wait for the promised infantry support before advancing. No infantry arrived.

Lord Raglan, meanwhile, could see the Russians recovering from the attack and regrouping. The worst thing was that they were able to steal British guns from the battlefield as they did so. He was furious, and dictated a second message to General Airey, which was immediately passed to a notorious hot-head named Captain Nolan. The second message read "Lord Raglan wishes the cavalry to advance rapidly to the front – follow the enemy and try to prevent the enemy carrying away the guns. Troop Horse Artillery may accompany, French cavalry is on your left. Immediate. Airey."

On receipt of this message, Lord Lucan thought through the

Chris Waddle is consoled by West Germany's captain

situation. The only guns he could see were situated at the far end of the valley in front of him and both he and Lord Cardigan, who was to lead the charge, could see that any charge towards them would result in the annihilation of the Light Brigade. It was death or glory. Death (politically) to ignore Lord Raglan's orders for a second time. Glory to send Lord Cardigan and his troops to certain death in the valley.

A hero would have seized the opportunity and stood up to his commanding officer on behalf of his men. Lucan fluffed and ordered the charge.

The first to die was Nolan, screaming like a lunatic at the head of the suicidal charge. *"C'est magnifique, mais ce n'est pas la guerre"* (It's fantastic but it's not war), said the French General Bosquet, watching from a nearby hill, *"C'est de la folie"* (it's madness).

Tiger Tiger, Burning Bright

In 1894 C. W. Allan was a well-known tiger hunter in Burma. On one occasion he was called to the village of Thinzin on forestry business to find that the village had been plagued by a man-eating tiger which had eaten two elephant drivers and a policeman in the previous six weeks. The villagers no longer dared to go into the forest but Allan rose to the challenge, as he recorded in his diary:

> On the morning of 18 March some twenty men turned up, and the Thugyi (village head man) informed me that the others would follow. So I made a move and got as far as the Khanpat stream, where I halted for a bit and had breakfast and then moved on again. It was my intention to make the Pyoungbok camp that day, as I was told it had a fence around it, made by the patrols to keep out the tiger. But the coolies would not move fast enough, so I camped on the Nanpalon stream.
>
> I turned into bed at about nine o' clock, and had not been in bed ten minutes when the clerk came and called me, saying that the tiger had come. I jumped

out of bed and taking my rifle I ran out. The men at
the fire told me that a pony tied near them began to
get very restless and kept looking towards the
stream, so they got up and looked and saw the
tiger not twenty paces off, ready to rush at them. I
asked them where it had gone to on being found out.
They replied that it had gone down into the stream.
   Whilst I was talking to the men, one man, who
was looking in the direction of the stream, said,
"look sir, there it is, going up the bank," and sure
enough there it was, about seventy yards off, going
across the bed of the stream. I had a shot and it
sprang up the bank, and just as it was disappearing I
fired a second shot. All the men said that I had hit it,
and Muang Kyaw Nay, my forester, was for going
and looking for blood, but I thought this too dangerous and would not let him go. The next morning
we got up early and went and had a look at the place
where the tiger had been standing when I fired at it. I
found where both the bullets had struck the ground.
They were both clean misses.

David Wilson, who reprinted Allan's story in his book *Anecdotes of Big Cats and Other Beasts* (London, 1910) makes excuses
for this simple technical error, stating that it is very hard to
shoot a tiger in the dark, even if you are the best shot in Burma,
as Allan was reputed to be. But Allan's diary continues to
develop in a way which only reinforces his ineptitude as a tiger-
hunter:

> On seeing the tiger was round our camp I took extra
> precautions and made all the men stop in one place
> just behind my tent; and gave orders to my Indian
> servants to have their dinner cooked early and to
> sleep with the Burmese coolies. My cook, an Indian,
> would not stop near the Burmese, though told to do
> so several times. He had his kitchen fire just in front
> of my tent. However I told him he must sleep with
> the other men. The other Indians also told him not to
> be a fool and stay away by himself. To them he
> replied that he was not afraid, and that if it was his
> fate the tiger would have him. He said "If it takes me,
> it will be a case of one crunch and all will be over."

He was, as things turned out, strictly accurate in his analysis.

> I was having dinner early (continues Allan), before it
> got quite dark, so as to get the men together. The
> cook had given me my soup and had cleared the
> plate and put a roast fowl before me and had gone
> back to the fire and was standing with a knife in his
> hand watching the pudding on the fire.
>
> I was just carving the chicken, when I heard the
> cook give a frightened cry, and on looking up I saw
> the tiger spring onto the cook. In jumping up I upset
> the table and the lamp on it and so it was dark again,
> just like the night before. I also upset a glass of beer
> that had just been poured out for me and I ran out
> shouting at the tiger and threw my table knife
> straight at his heart. Unfortunately I missed. My
> dogs, two terriers and a spaniel, were sitting by
> my table and they all jumped up and ran after the
> tiger with me and also attacked it. One terrier and
> the spaniel were killed on the spot and the other dog
> limped away. In spite of this onslaught, the tiger
> went off with the cook. I thought the tiger had got
> the cook by the back, but the sweeper, who was
> standing close by with my goats, said it had got him
> by the head, and so it turned out to be the case.

Allan did eventually get another shot at the tiger but again
without success and the next morning (after several more
unsuccessful attempts to locate the animal) they went into
the forest to retrieve the body of the cook.

> The tiger had caught the cook by the head, as the
> sweeper had said, for one fang had gone into his
> right eye and knocked it out, another had gone into
> his throat just below the chin and two had gone into
> the skull and neck at the back. So it must have taken
> the whole head into its mouth for it was a pulp with
> the brains coming out.

And so it seems that the cook's forecast of his own unfortunate
demise was the only part of the scheme that went right. Allan
arranged for a shallow grave to be dug for the cook and took his
coolies out of the forest without a moment's delay. One year

later, however, he returned to the same spot with his new wife, to show her the scene and to pay his respects at the cook's grave. The tiger was still at large.

Shooting Yourself in the Foot

Tony Price of the rock group *Revolver* was on holiday in Israel in 1969 when his car was hijacked. The armed hitchhiker recognised the rock-star immediately and realised that a golden kidnap opportunity had fallen into his lap. He pointed his gun at Price and told him to drive straight ahead or else. Amazed, Price drove directly into the huge pile of sand immediately in front of the car and, in the ensuing confusion, the gun went off. But, instead of giving any further orders, the gunman simply screamed and fell out of the car. He had committed the perfect mistake of shooting himself in the foot.

England Expects

It was 4 July 1990. Partly due to luck and partly due to talent, England had got further than ever before on foreign soil in the football World Cup. Never had the televisual hopes of so many hung on the trainers of so few – except for the Bruno–Tyson match but that doesn't count.

Germany were favourites. They had been finalists in the last two tournaments and they hadn't needed extra time in any of their matches this year. They were managed by one of the world's all-time greatest players, Franz Beckenbauer, who declared that victory was by no means a foregone conclusion since England were always a team of two halves and, anyway, now they had Gazza. English fans everywhere were desperate to see their team in the final against Argentina since it was

Marradona's 'Hand of God' which had painfully destroyed them the last time round.

The scene was set. Thirty million British people were tuned in. The sky was bright blue. England *could* win. Via Gazza, Wright, Waddle and Beardsley England won the first three corners. Everything was looking good. Winning is about self-belief and, thank heavens, at last Robson's men had acquired some. Voller, a German striker, fell to the floor and Beckenbauer's Boys were down to ten men. Gazza was here, there and everywhere. He tousled Brehme's hair indulgently, he knew he was on to a winner. The first half whistle blew.

Fifty-nine minutes in and Hassler took a free kick which deflected off Paul Parker and went over Shilton. One–nil to Germany. But England weren't to be beaten that easily. Twenty minutes left and Lineker, running forward to meet a cross from the indefatigable Parker, met the ball, fired and scored. Everyone went mad. The tension was unbearable. Extra time and Platt put the ball in the net. Offside. Disallowed. After two hours all play time was used up. It was still one all. The applause was deafening but this is a game of two teams and one team had to lose. The unthinkable was about to happen. With Gazza crying and Robson, back in London, ashen-faced and tearful, penalty shoot-out began.

Lineker scored, of course. Every man, woman and household pet in Britain held its breath. Peter Shilton made the right decision, dived with gusto but couldn't get his hand to the ball. Brehme scored. Beardsley scored, then Matthaus; Platt and then Riedle. Three all. Illgner saved the shot from Pearce who walked away in silence, the audience stunned. Thon scored and then . . . and then it was all up to Chris Waddle. The man with the worst hairdo on the pitch had the heart of England on his mud-stained shoes. And he missed.

It was the mistake to end all footballing mistakes. Chris Waddle couldn't kick a ball into an open goal and England weren't going to go to the final.

chapter two

ERRORS OF JUDGEMENT

M istake category 2. *We all have those moments when we have to make snap judgements about the people we meet and the things we do. We all have those moments when we get them wrong.*

Sex and Hitler

Having rigorously researched all available historical knowledge, I am confidently able to reveal that it was definitively a mistake to fall in love with Hitler. The German dictator is officially on record as having had sex with nine women, seven of whom died immediately after the event.

He started his romantic career with a neurotic fear of syphilis which resulted in chronic impotency during his youthful years and he was only cured by a long and strenuous process of psychotherapy. He had no lovers at all during his boyhood: the one man who ever claimed to be a friend of Adolf's, August Kubizek, recorded for posterity that Hitler "hardly noticed ladies' encouraging glances, or, at most, would make an annoyed comment to me about them." This was not an illustrious start to a career as the most devastating Don Juan of Berlin.

In 1921, aged thirty-two, he acquired his first girlfriend, Suzi Liptauer. She was the first of many identikit ladies – all blonde, all half his age, all athletic and all (except Magda Goebbels) personally unambitious. We can only speculate on what happened in that Viennese damsel's bedroom but, after their single night of physical interaction, Suzi hanged herself and Hitler withdrew from the sexual battlefield for seven years. In 1928, now thirty-nine, he began a two year love affair with Maria Reiter, aged sixteen. He then dumped her and she hanged herself from a clothes line attached to a door-handle in the family home.

Hitler's libido was obviously picking up speed. Less than a year later, aged forty, he encouraged his niece, Geli Rambal, aged nineteen, to come and live with him in his flat in Vienna. This was a bad move for Geli. Being locked up all day by her uncle, forced to have sex at will and having her every move guarded by the Gestapo was not her idea of a teenage love-affair. She tried to leave the flat and, quite accidentally, she happened to die in the process. The Ministry of Justice refused Hitler's half-sister's request for an investigation.

Hitler, though lovelorn, immediately found a new girlfriend, Martha Dodd. She was the daughter of William Dodd, the US ambassador to Berlin. Adolf was quite keen on Martha, much to the chagrin of Goring who thought that consorting with the potential enemy was just not cricket. He had her investigated and was soon in possession of a whole dossier of unflattering material which he presented to the nobbing Nazi. Hitler didn't care a jot about the fact that she had been arrested for drunk and disorderly in her native Chicago, nor was he interested in the fact that she had got divorced a mere two months after her wedding. But on hearing that her father had taught history at the University of Chicago, which, at that time, was reputed to be a hotbed of Communist activity, he totally flipped and immediately threw her out. Martha was devastated and slashed her wrists. She survived and, relieved of her US passport for having consorted with the ultimate enemy, she had little choice but to disappear behind the Iron Curtain.

Goebbels, the Minister for Public Enlightenment, felt Adolf needed a little paternal guidance in his love life. He would choose the leader's next girlfriend for him, thus eliminating all possible unsavoury after-tastes. Having scanned through his official lists of German Beauties, lucky Renate Muller, a film star, was the next one up on the Hitler score sheet. Renate herself was the only person who wasn't keen on the plan. She was flown to Berlin in a private plane. She was sent flowers every day and then, when that didn't work, diamonds and then furs. Goebbels arranged for glowing reviews of her performances to be published in what were now effectively his private national newspapers. Before Goebbels' well-known less subtle tactics were employed, Renate, a sensible girl, got the hint. Adolf was on for more.

Meanwhile, back at the ranch, Renate had, unfortunately for her, fallen in love with a Jewish businessman. They waited till the sexual coast was clear for a few days and then they legged it. The Gestapo weren't that stupid. The couple were caught at the border and taken back to Berlin where Renate was forced to whip her boyfriend to death in front of her mocking captors. She then, quite accidentally, fell from a third-floor window and died.

Adolf was really building up phallic steam and couldn't wait for more. Enter Stage Left – Unity Mitford, the daughter of Lord Redesdale. Eva Braun, who by this stage had started interacting with Adolf the Sexgod, records her despair at the affair in 1935

Eva Braun with Hitler

in her diary. But Hitler was keen to use his English girlfriend as a propaganda agent. Her parents were friends with Churchill and Anthony Eden. When she went home, the stars of love in her eyes, she greeted all her old friends with the endearing words "Heil Hitler" and did the Nazi salute. She wore a swastika constantly and displayed photos of herself on the arms of her beloved Adolf.

She went back to Germany in 1939 where she was introduced as "Lady" Mitford, which she was not. On 3 September war was declared and she realised that she had been duped and made a laughing stock. Boldly she went into the nearest government office and demanded to see her boyfriend. She was told to leave the country immediately. She went outside the building and promptly shot herself. She survived, suffering crippling brain damage, and was taken to hospital where friends of Adolf's brought her cheering souvenirs including a metal swastika which she immediately swallowed. This attempt, too, failed. She was shipped back to England and confined to prison as a seditious war criminal. Then she died.

By 1943 the war wasn't going too well. Hitler picked up Inge Ley for refreshment purposes but, immediately post-coital, she took the rather drastic but by this stage predictable step of jumping out of the bedroom window to her death.

We are only left now with the obvious two. Eva Braun was completely potty about Herr Hitler and daily inscribed in her journal the prayer "Dear God, please make it possible to let me see him today". It wasn't always possible, of course, since he was often engaged in alternative sexual acts or, occasionally, genocide. During their seventeen-year relationship, Eva attempted suicide twice. It was a particular problem that her long-standing live-in lover would never acknowledge that she existed. Eventually she swallowed a cyanide capsule in the bunker alongside the love of her life. Two hours later Magda Goebbels, the wife of the aforementioned 'Enlightenment Joe', chose to poison her six children in this very same bunker and then top herself to boot. She could never have been happy without him.

The Bay of Pigs

One of the most bungled military operations of all time was
America's attempt under the leadership of John F. Kennedy to
get rid of Fidel Castro, the maverick Communist leader of
Cuba. The plan had been conceived by President Eisenhower as
a vote winner towards the end of his term of office but the
Republicans lost the election. One of the first decisions JFK
made when he came to office was to go ahead with it all the
same. This was the first of many errors of judgement in the Bay
of Pigs affair.

The prime favourable aspect of the plan was that there were
hundreds of Cuban political defectors in the US and they all
wanted to overthrow Castro. The CIA, under Richard Bissell,
had trained them as a crack guerrilla force especially for this
purpose. A deal was made with Roberto Alejo, the brother of
the Guatemalan ambassador, to take over his coffee plantation
and train the lads there. Paratroopers made practise jumps in
Florida since the entire scheme revolved around the early and
surprise destruction of the Cuban air force by a team which
would be making round trip flights from an air base 500 miles
away. The go-ahead for landing was given to Trinidad beach,
which was open country leading directly to the main guerrilla
encampment.

Washington then made a large number of military mistakes,
the most important being its lack of understanding of human
nature. Every single one of the guerrilla leaders wanted to be in
control of the operation. They all fought like mad for control of
events and were so busy deciding who should be in charge that
the operation itself was forgotten and the deadline for organi-
sation expired. Delay was a bad mistake. The guerrillas waiting
to be met in the mountains were located, as everyone knew
they would be eventually, and arrested. So that was the first
major problem area – the whole scheme had been devised
around a link-up procedure and now there was no-one to link
up with.

JFK simultaneously became obsessed with public opinion.
Trinidad was heavily populated and he didn't think an invasion there would go down very well with the press – which is
not generally considered a factor to take into account if you are
considering military success – so he swapped the landing to the

Bay of Pigs which was much less carefully researched. He also thought it might help with the media if the coup happened at night – not taking into account that it was a long time since some of the refugees had actually lived in Cuba and they might well not find their way around in the darkness. And then he couldn't really decide whether the whole thing was a good idea or not. He committed the fatal military mistake of falling between two stools. Grudgingly he gave his consent to the operation but imposed conditions which meant it could never succeed. US forces were not to be involved in landing and air strikes were only to be led by Cuban pilots, who couldn't fly properly, taking off from Guatemala, which was too far away. The Joint Chiefs of Staff pointed out that the rebels were bound to be defeated but JFK overruled them.

Finally there was only one element left which could herald victory and that was surprise. As the flotilla of seven ships prepared to set sail from Nicaragua on 17 April 1961, and all the locals and newspapermen turned up to see what was going on, the Nicaraguan president, Samoza, appeared on the dock and called out loudly and repeatedly "Bring me a couple of hairs from Castro's beard." This was not a good idea.

The first frogman ashore swam straight into a military patrol. The under-researched landing point, the Bay of Pigs, turned out to be the construction site of a new luxury resort, and as the soldiers landed, they were greeted by a large number of cheery workmen driving tractors. Finally the CIA had thought that the Bay of Pigs was a sandy beach whereas, in fact, it was full of pebbles and, as the frogmen emerged from the waves, they all hit themselves against the rocks, whilst several of the dinghies had their hulls gutted and sank.

The worst mistake of all for what was meant to be a surprise attack, of course, is that Castro knew they were coming. As the invaders emerged they were picked up one by one and arrested. All the waiting boats panicked and sailed away leaving the men on the beaches without supplies and with no means of escape. Castro's forces took hundreds of prisoners and by 19 April, the planned coup had ended in utter humiliation. Castro was jubilant and made lots of extra revenue for his country by leading groups of interested tourists around the weapon-strewn beaches.

Of course not all category 2 mistakes are so costly . . .

Sick Bag

In 1976 British Aircraft Corporation made a bad mistake before they had even got off the ground. They decided to produce a safety film for the workers at their Preston factory which would impress upon the staff the need to wear protective goggles at all times. The effects of being educated were so powerful that, during the screening of this short educational film, thirteen members of staff had to be carried out of the room by fellow workers and nursing staff. In one particularly gruesome moment of *cinema verité*, a welder fell off his chair and subsequently needed seven stitches. Later a group of machine engineers, who had hitherto been considered hardy, strapping fellows, had to be led out of the room, nauseous and trembling.

The film was shortly afterwards withdrawn for safety reasons.

Peace in Our Time

Probably the most embarrassing political mistake of the century was believing Adolf Hitler.

On 14 September 1938 Neville Chamberlain, the British Prime Minister at the time, flew to meet the German Chancellor at Godesburg where Hitler politely informed the British Prime Minister that Sudetenland was to be taken over in its entirety by German troops. Not surprisingly the British, French and Czech leaders were not entirely happy with this proposal and on 27 September British troops were told to get ready for war.

By the end of September matters were looking desperate. The Prime Ministers of Britain, France and Italy all met Hitler in Munich in order to solve what had become a tricky issue. Since the Czechs were the main stumbling block to achieving some kind of settlement with the Germans, the leaders had the brilliant military idea of leaving them out of the peace talks entirely. It was much easier then to formulate a scheme whereby German troops were permitted to occupy Sudetenland on 1 October with the new borders to be decided by a four-power commission not to include the Czechs. Chamberlain was very pleased with this sophisticated piece of negotiation and persuaded Hitler to sign a brief note declaring "the desire of our two peoples never to go to war with one another again".

On 1 October 1938, Neville Chamberlain flew home from Munich to a frenzied welcome from thousands of Londoners, flourishing his piece of paper and declaring to ten thousand people at Heston airport that "I believe it is peace for our time." The Prime Minister's welcome at Downing Street was overrun by women crying and screaming out "thank you, thank you", whilst policemen valiantly held back the jubilantly thronging masses.

"I want to say," said Neville Chamberlain, "that the settlement of the Czechoslovak problem is only a prelude to a larger settlement in which all Europe may find peace." Crowds accompanied his progress all the way to Buckingham Palace singing "for he's a jolly good fellow". The *Daily Herald* reported that whilst Czechoslovakia might lose its mines, its timber belts and most of its famous spa towns, the Czechs would probably be satisfied since they would not lose their world-renowned Pilsen brewery.

Under a year later, on 3 September 1939, Poland was invaded by the combined military might of Germany and Russia and Britain declared war, followed rapidly by France. Winston Churchill took over immediately as First Lord of the Admiralty and, very shortly afterwards, Neville Chamberlain had no choice but to resign.

Teething Problems

Woman's Weekly – 28 June 1924

Dear Aunt Agatha
I am very worried, and am writing to you for help and advice. I have kept company with a man for three years. We have been unable to marry because

he has an aged mother to keep and there is not very much money. All the time however we have been a great deal to each other and have looked forward to saving enough to marry and support her, too. Just lately, however, I have had my teeth out and got false ones. Since then his manner to me has changed and he passes slighting remarks on my appearance and makes me feel very uncomfortable. I am now 35. Do you think his love will outlast old age and fading looks?
Worried Ada.

Ada, my dear, you have asked me the most poignant question that one woman can ask another. That he can be so unkind as to make slighting remarks on your appearance conclusively proves that he is entirely lacking in nice feeling. I cannot think that such a man would make a kind or sympathetic husband. What would he be like, or how would he act to you in sickness or trouble ? You may think it a hard thing to be an old maid – but, Ada, my dear, it is a much harder thing to be the wife of an unkind and sneering husband. Think over this aspect of the matter and bring your common sense and good judgement to bear on the subject. Then make up your mind as to what to do.
Yours Aunt Agatha

To Have and to Hold Down

Lord Roberts began his military career as a quarter-master general in India in 1860 but he was very ambitious and was very much hoping to be asked to join the regiment which was being formed to wipe out the Taku forts. Much to Roberts' chagrin, two soldiers called Lumsden and Allgood, however, were chosen instead.

A few days later he and his new wife were invited to dinner by the very Lord Clyde who had been in charge of choosing who was to go on the expedition. Lord Clyde looked very pleased with himself and insisted on taking the arm of the new Lady Roberts and escorting her into dinner. As he did so he asked her earnestly if she was not about to thank him profusely for his pains. Lady Roberts looked mystified and asked him, tartly, which pains it was that he thought that he had taken.

"Why for not sending your husband with the expedition, of course" replied the chivalrous Lord Clyde – always the romantic at heart. If Roberts had not just been married, he explained, he would have been the obvious person to send. Lady Roberts, who was almost as ambitious as her husband, retorted brusquely "I am afraid I cannot be very grateful to you for making my husband feel I am ruining his career by standing in the way of his being sent on service. You have done your best to make him regret his marriage."

The Commander-in-Chief was frankly astonished. "I'll be hanged if I can understand you women!" he exclaimed. "I have done the very thing I thought you would like, and have only succeeded in making you angry. I will never try to help a woman again." And he never did.

Charles and Diana:
The Fireside Story

Are you sitting comfortably? Then I'll begin.

She was a Cancer; he was an Aquarius – it could never have worked. She had no "O" levels, no skills and a lot of money. He had a degree from Cambridge, no skills and even more money.

They met on a hay bale in West Sussex at a barbeque and they talked about loneliness and loss – something of which they were both about to experience a great deal. He took her to see Verdi's *Requiem*. They fell in love. The rest is history.

• chapter three •

PIGHEADEDNESS

M istake category 3. Certain mistakes derive from personality *flaws. One of the most common is pigheadedness. Intransigence, inability to take advice from others, smugness and the habit of snorting are usual accompanying characteristics. You probably know a few pigheads yourself. You can list them in the pighead chart at the end of this chapter.*

Pighead Walpole

When Brigadier "Pighead" Walpole set off to take the Fort Ruiya during the Indian Mutiny in 1858, there seemed to be no cause for alarm. It was a simple mopping-up operation and even though the Brigadier had a reputation for stubbornness and stupidity, it seemed impossible that he would have any problems. This proved to be a mistake.

On his way to the fort, Pighead had an unexpected stroke of luck. He met a British soldier who had just escaped from the fort with the information that there were only 200 men inside and that Nirpat Singh, their commander, intended to offer token resistance and then to surrender.

Walpole decided to ignore this information. He also refused to listen to the soldier's description of the fort lay-out or to send out a reconnaissance party to plot the best direction of attack. Any reconnaissance at all would have shown that the fort was practically impossible to defend, because its rear wall was only a few feet high. Singh's plan to surrender was, in the circumstances, the only reasonable course of action he could have taken. When he saw the massed British troops approaching the massive front wall of the fort, however, he changed his mind – as soon as he'd got over the shock. With his tiny band of men, he poured fire down on the advancing regiments inflicting heavy losses. Walpole, convinced by now that there were at least 1,500 men in the fort, panicked and called a retreat.

That night, Nirpat Singh retreated with all his 200 men, leaving red-faced Walpole to attack an empty fort the next day.

Bloody-Minded Bard

The brilliant eighteenth-century Irish playwright Richard Brinsley Sheridan was as stubborn as a mule. When he was choosing the cast for his play *The Critic*, Sheridan was absolutely insistent that the minor role of Lord Burghley should be played by a notoriously stupid actor called John Moody. Everyone pleaded with him to leave Moody out, but Sheridan insisted. The role was so simple, he said, that no-one could possibly make a mistake in it. The plucky playwright was so confident that he made a wager with the theatre manager that everything would pass off without a hitch.

Things were trickier in the theatre then than they are now, because there was almost no time allowed for rehearsal. The stage directions were carefully written and smaller parts would often be played for the first time on the opening night. Lord Burghley had no lines to speak. He just had to sit for a while on-stage and obey the single stage direction "Lord Burghley comes forward, pauses near Dangle, shakes his head, and exits." Nonetheless, Sheridan took special care with Moody. He personally read him the direction, told him where to sit, and left him to familiarise himself with the part.

When the grand moment arrived, Sheridan and the manager were on tenter-hooks. Sure enough, Moody got up from his seat at exactly the right moment and, realising that his reputation depended on it, made his way steadily forwards to where Dangle was standing. Then he reached out his hands to the sides of Dangle's head, shook it gently, smiled contentedly at the audience and wandered back to the wings.

Colonel Custer – a Hog

One of the youngest generals in the Union Army, George Armstrong Custer (1839-1876) was considered to be an extremely talented military man and given command of all expeditions into Indian territories after the Civil War had ended.

On 25 June 1876, he was thrilled to discover a large Indian encampment at Little Bighorn in Montana and determined to make his fame and fortune in one fell swoop. Custer failed to take account of the fact that the Indians were led by two of their all-time greatest leaders, the legendary Sitting Bull and Crazy Horse. This was a bad mistake. Custer charged into a full frontal attack on the natives in which he and every single one of his soldiers were ingloriously annihilated.

The scene of what has become known as Custer's Last Stand is now a national monument. Amongst his peers, Custer was generally considered to be a rather arrogant fellow.

Pighead Chart

add your own pigheads to the list

Name	intransigence	advice resistance	smugness	snorting rate
Walpole	moderate	very high	too stupid	enormous
Sheridan	high	very high	also high	strangely low
Custer	extreme	too isolated	yes	unknown

• chapter four •

EGO ALL OVER YOUR FACE

*T*oo big for your own boots, and then they trip you up. That's what happens to victims of mistake category 4. Posers and Boasters and above all Egomaniacs are the characters for this chapter. See if you can tell them apart from the Pigheads.

Nongqawuse – the Xhosa Prophetess

Nongqawuse was only fourteen years old but she was a very persuasive teenager. In 1856 she sat staring into the Gxara river and considered that she had received the call of her forebears.

On returning to her village in a semi-ecstatic state, she declared herself to be the liberator of her people whose ancestors had told her that they were just about ready to rise up from the dead and lead their descendants into an undeniably victorious war against the colonial Europeans who were taking over everywhere.

The Gcaleka Xhosa leaders were very pleased to hear this news and asked Nongqawuse what they should do to assist the planned rebellion. Well, she said, they would have to prove their devotion to the cause by burning all their crops, slaughtering all their livestock and destroying any worldly possessions that might remain lying around. The Xhosas couldn't really win on this one since they were also informed that, were they not to do this, they would be destroyed by a plague of man-eating locusts.

The Xhosas spent the entire year getting ready for their big day and on 18 February 1857, they stood out in the fields waiting for the miracle to happen. Nongqawuse told them that, for the first time in the history of mankind, the sun would turn on its tail at midday and return to set in the east, thus heralding the dawn of the new age. The tribesmen stared and stared, and they didn't have sunglasses in those days, but the sun just carried on its normal arc and, finally, sank down over the horizon in the west. This was rather a blow for Nongqawuse who realised immediately that, having burnt all their goods and having nothing left to eat for their supper that night, this was very likely to be her. She ran away and sought refuge with the very people she had been keen to annihilate a few hours earlier and the British placed her, for her own safety, on Robben Island where she assumed a new identity and became a farmer, dying peaceably in 1898.

The Xhosa tribe were not so fortunate. Twenty-five thousand died of hunger.

Straight from the Hart

"I know I am going to be President" said Senator Gary "Bigmouth" Hart.

San Domingo's Hero

Born into slavery in 1743, Toussaint L'Ouverture was a serf for over fifty years on a West Indian plantation before he led his

native island of San Domingo (now Haiti) to glorious revolt
and subsequent independence. His career was flourishing until
the time at which he made the fatal (and common) political
mistake of self-aggrandisement. He had himself officially
declared the new Napoleon, which didn't go down too well
with the old one, who was still very much alive.

Toussaint's father, Gaou Guinou, was the son of an African
chief who, having been captured in a civil war with a neighbouring tribe, was sold to a slave-trader who transported him
to Haiti. Here he married a fellow slave and had several
children, of whom Toussaint was the eldest. From his earliest
years the boy displayed great intelligence and rose quickly
through the social ranks from his humble position of shepherd
to that of coachman and eventually to being appointed overseer
of his master's plantation. He got married to Suzanne Simon
and had two sons. The couple were obviously very happy; he
wrote in his memoirs that "we went to work in the fields, my
wife and I, hand in hand". He read a great deal and was
particularly interested in a tract which Diderot, the French
philosopher, had written as an indictment of slavery. It contained the words "Your slaves need a chief sufficiently coura-
geous to lead them to vengeance and slaughter. Where is this
great man to be found? Where is this new Spartacus ? He will
appear, we cannot doubt it; he will show himself to raise the
sacred standard of Liberty." Toussaint was absolutely convinced that the words were a personal message for him. He
was the Spartacus who would deliver his people from their
fetters.

He carefully shipped out his wife and children to a place of
safety before he hastened to join the forces who were preparing
themselves to revolt against their colonialist oppressors. He
was a man of simple tastes; his daily diet consisted of a few
oatmeal cakes and bananas, whilst he only ever drank water.
He never slept more than two hours a night and, during the
seven years in which he was engaged in active fighting, he was
wounded 19 times. Both he and his followers began to consider
him inhuman and everyone treated him as such. He inspired
exceptional loyalty in his generals – Rigaud the mulatto,
Dessalines the brutal and Christophe the brave – and he was
never guilty of inflicting unnecessary cruelty on defeated
parties. Under his brilliant leadership San Domingo was led
to independence and Toussaint took the name of "L'Ouverture" (the opening), demonstrating his intention of opening to

his followers the brighter future which they had always been denied.

In 1797, France realised that Toussaint was in an unassailable military position and, making the best of a bad job, they appointed him Commander-in-Chief and went home. Toussaint was left in supreme control and, in 1798, the first thing he did, after abolishing slavery, was to proclaim a general amnesty and invite all the refugee land-owners to return home. Toussaint considered that sudden unaccustomed liberty might corrupt his people and so he decreed that for five years emancipated slaves must continue to work for their old masters, receiving in payment a quarter of the produce of their toil during the term of the apprenticeship.

So far so good. But all the power began to go to Toussaint's head. He set up a splendid court and wore a uniform which was a close imitation of Napoleon's own, including the distinctive hat and feather. He was always preceded by two trumpeters and an escort of guards. He held special imperial style ceremonies at which everyone present except himself had

Francis Pym MP, Minister of Defence

to stand and maintain a respectful attitude while he circled around the room, speaking to each of his subjects in turn. He began to make speeches in Latin, which he had learnt by heart from the Psalter and which was utterly meaningless but which he considered an impressive display of learning. And then, finally, he declared repeatedly and seriously that "I am the new Buonaparte of San Domingo and the colony could not exist without me." When the French ambassador arrived in a ship from Paris, he was none too pleased with this state of affairs and asked Toussaint to accompany him back to France in order to explain himself to Napoleon. "Your ship, sir," replied Toussaint scornfully, "is not big enough for a man like me."

This was a mistake. Napoleon heard of Toussaint's disdain almost immediately and sent a fleet to retake the colony, declaring Toussaint to be "a revolting slave who must be suitably punished and brought to his senses". Toussaint's fate was not assisted by the fact that Napoleon, at that time, was married to Josephine who was a native of Martinique, another French Caribbean island, and hated the neighbouring people of San Domingo as a matter of course. Toussaint knew that resistance was useless. The whole of the French navy had been sent to destroy the man who had dared to claim himself the New Napoleon. His men deserted him and he had no choice but to surrender himself to the French leader "This is what men are like," he said, "I have seen them at my feet, these people who now insult me. But it will not be long before they regret me."

He was seized, put in irons and taken to a dungeon in the Jura mountain range in France, where he spent the remaining days of his life in the composition of pathetic appeals to Napoleon himself addressed "from the first of the blacks to the first of the whites". He died eighteen months later, a broken man, but his memory lives on in the poetry of Wordsworth, who wrote these words in honour of one who, had he not made the tragic mistake of self-importance, could have died a happy man:

> There's not a breathing of the common wind
> That will forget him; he hath great allies;
> His friends are exultations, agonies
> And love, and man's unconquerable mind!

Fingerlickin' Good

When France fell to the Germans in the Second World War, General Weyland said "In three weeks England will have her neck wrung like a chicken." It was to this remark that Churchill famously replied "Some Chicken. Some Neck."

Wets

In June 1983, Foreign Secretary Francis Pym went live on TV saying that too big a Conservative majority in the General Election would be bad for the country. He was sacked within forty-eight hours.

• chapter five •

THE MOCKING JAWS OF FATE

*V*ictims of mistake category 5 are people who fall into "the mocking jaws of fate". They can't help it. They didn't do anything wrong. But they got it in the head. Or, like General Grant's sperm donor, in the gooly.

Ging Gang Gooly Gooly Gooly Gooly Gotcha!

During the American Civil War an unusual military mistake was recorded by the medical journal, the *Lancet* in 1875.

A badly aimed bullet was seen to penetrate the left testicle of one of General Grant's soldiers and, having passed straight through, flew on to lodge itself in the stomach of a young volunteer nurse.

Nine months later she gave birth to an eight-pound baby boy. Her GP, one Dr L. G. Capers of Missouri, confirmed that she was indeed still a woman of unimpeachable sexual reputation. He had never encountered an immaculate conception before and was therefore intrigued on being called to the baby's bed some few weeks later in order to operate on a swelling in its side. Having removed a large piece of shrapnel he put two and two together and concluded that the bullet which had hit the soldier had carried some sperm with it and impregnated his lady patient.

Dr Capers was a man of initiative. At once he set off to locate the missing father, found him, brought him back to Missouri and introduced the pair who fell in love and, unusually for this book, got married and lived happily ever after.

Flower of Scotland

In 1739 the Russians and the Turks, who had been at war with each other for some considerable time, finally decided to declare a truce. The two sides sent their respective commissioners to negotiate a full and final settlement which would be agreeable to both parties. Both of these men – that is Marshal Keith for the Russians and the Grand Vizier for the Turks – were eminent military men in their fields and the serious negotiations were begun by means of interpreters.

Many hours later, after laborious translations had been undertaken on all sides, the deal was concluded and the two commissioners finally got up to leave. Suddenly the Grand Vizier marched over to Marshal Keith and grabbed him by the hand, which he shook forcibly, and told him, in the broadest Scotch accent that he was "unco" happy to meet a countryman in his exalted station. Keith was astonished and stared at the Turkish diplomat.

The Grand Vizier told him not to be surprised and, smiling broadly, he added "I'm o' the same country wi' yoursell, mon! I mind weel seeing you and your brother, when boys, passin' by to the school at Kirkaldy; my father, sir, was bellman o' Kirkaldy."

Titanic

Captain E.J. Smith was on his very last sea voyage. It was the very first to be undertaken by the brand new mega-ship the *Titanic*. Although not big by today's standards, the Titanic had a capacity of just under 3,400 passengers and was aiming to set a new Southampton–New York speed record on its maiden voyage. Captain Smith was almost 60 and declared to his sister as the ship set sail that "The sea is not wet enough to drown me. I'll never be drowned". This overconfidence in the supervessel was, quite patently, a mistake.

Once the iceberg which was the cause of the disaster was spotted, the engines on the boat were reversed, which was, possibly, also a mistake. Had they not been, it is possible that the blow would merely have crumpled the fore peak and caused no more inconvenience than the flooding of the number one hold. But this is a matter for speculation.

Thomas Andrew, the builder and designer of the Titanic, had calculated that if the damage had not extended beyond four out of the six compartments in the bulkhead, the ship would have remained afloat. In fact it extended as far as the sixth compartment, which meant that the vessel was doomed. The fact that the engines had been reversed meant that the ship also came to a rapid halt in the middle of an extremely icy ocean and, with due deference to the number of celebrated wealthy people on board and to his own unsinkability, Captain Smith had omitted to run through the traditional emergency drill procedure.

Closest of all nearby vessels was the *Carpathia*, but her only radio operator was off duty. Fortunately for the Titanic he just happened to call in to the Titanic before he went to bed to ask about traffic conditions in Cape Cod. On hearing the news, the Carpathia went directly to the Titanic and by 8:30 in the morning the last of the survivors had been rescued. 705 of the 2,200 passengers had been rescued and those missing included Thomas Andrews, the designer, and Captain Smith.

At the Senate Inquiry which was later held to establish the facts of the case, the vice-president of the company that owned the boat, White Star, cited its company rule 101:

> Commanders must distinctly understand that the
> issue of these regulations does not in any way

relieve them from the responsibility for the safe and efficient navigation of their respective vessels, and they are also enjoined to remember that they must run no risk which might by any possibility result in an accident to their ship.

Despite these incredibly specific injunctions, it was common knowledge that Captain Smith consistently maintained full speed under conditions similar to those on 12 April. In his favour, a very large number of experienced Captains did testify that this was current practice and no-one could be found who was prepared to condemn the drowned Captain. But the Board of Inquiry stated:

> He made a mistake, a very grievous mistake, but one in which, in face of the practice and past experience, negligence cannot be said to have had any part; and, in the absence of negligence it is . . . impossible to fix Captain Smith with blame.

Props Department

The props department at the ancient Globe Theatre pulled out all the stops for the opening night of Shakespeare's play *Henry VIII* on 29 June 1613. One of their more interesting ideas was to use real cannons to greet the entrance of the lusty king, even though the theatre was built entirely of wood with a thatched roof.

At the beginning of a big scene in Cardinal Wolsey's house, one of the cannons missed its aim slightly and a lump of red-hot wadding got caught in the straw roof of the theatre. According to Sir Henry Wotton, who was there at the time, the audience was so engrossed in the play that no-one noticed a thing until the whole theatre was in flames and was burnt to the ground within an hour.

Remarkably no-one seems to have died in the blazing inferno. "Only one man had his breeches set on fire", said Wotton in a letter to his nephew, "which would perhaps have broiled him, if he had not put it out with a bottle of ale". I bet he drank Carling Black Label.

Pier Pressure

On 13 February 1979 Britain's leading architects met at Skegness Pier to hand over an award for best designed pier theatre to a very talented fellow called George Sunderland.

During the presentation ceremony a storm broke and the theatre was swept out to sea.

What's Up Doc?

The jazz musician, Matty Matlock, was playing golf on the island of Catalina when he hit a wild drive on to another fairway and knocked out a passing pedestrian. Matlock was wild with remorse and ran around shouting "Doctor, doctor, find me a doctor". "You're very lucky", said a local passer-by. "We only have one doctor on this island and he happens to be playing golf this very day. In fact that's him over there, lying flat on his back in the middle of the fairway".

A Dip off the Old Block

John Helms, a young but unsuccessful New York artist, was depressed. It was Christmas Eve 1977, he was all alone and no-one wanted to buy his paintings. He climbed to the 86th Floor of the Empire State Building and made up his mind to end it all. Without any more ado he prepared to meet his end and flung himself from the observation tower onto which he had emerged.

Half an hour later he woke up to discover that, in fact, he had fallen just two and a half feet, landing on a ledge somewhere between the 86th and 85th Floor. A somewhat surprised television engineer, Bill Steckman, looked up from his work to see John knocking at his window and asking to be let in. Bill poured himself a stiff drink, opened the window and John was saved.

This mistaken endeavour had a very happy ending for Mr Helms. On news being broadcast of his lack of success, thousands of people all over America rang him up to offer him a home and a meal for Christmas lunch. Mr Helms was convinced that he had been meant to survive and, wisely, accepted.

Key Positions

In November 1983 a night-club boss and local gang leader, Jimmy "the Beard" Ferrozo, was engaged in a sex romp at one of his clubs, The Condor, with a twenty-three year old stripper called Teresa Hill.

As they writhed around on the top of the club's baby grand piano, after closing hours, Teresa's spine came into contact with the button that caused the piano to rise up slowly from the floor. Jimmy and Teresa were otherwise occupied and didn't notice their sudden rise in status. The romp ended quite suddenly as the piano reached the ceiling. Miss Hill screamed for help and firemen arrived to rescue the unfulfilled couple. Teresa was pulled out, naked and bruised. But Jimmy was already dead.

Dead on Arrival

The ninth President of the United States, William Henry Harrison, was inaugurated after an enormous amount of to-do, on 4 March 1841. He died of pneumonia on 4 April.

Harrison resembles Pope John Paul I (the Hippy Pope) in this respect, who was given the Catholic top-job in the late seventies and died after only a month in office. There was a big hoo-ha at the time which was completely hushed up. The word was that the trendy pontiff had been bumped off by Vatican conservatives who wanted Rome to have a less flexible vicar.

Fire Fire

It was a hot day in Henley. A fire broke out in the locality and the occupants of the worst hit house telephoned the local fire brigade who were all "indisposed" since they were taking part in a simulated fire drill on an imaginary inferno miles away.

Distressed, the occupants called the next nearest fire station, which wasn't near at all. Some time later an engine came crawling up the local hill which was all too much for its ancient parts. The cab burst into flames and the firemen clambered out, spewing up all over the pavement. It was then impossible to use the suction pump since it was all clogged up with smoke.

Quite by chance, the local fire engine just then happened to come tootling past and stopped to see what was going on. They were, however, unable actually to assist since they had no water left on board having just used it all up and in the process waterlogging the village green on which they had just been practising their dummy run.

Whilst the first and second fire crews stopped passing motorists and asked them to help put out the fire in the engine, all the locals got together and put out the fire in the house using that well-known fire-fighting device, running up and down with buckets.

Star-Struck

A commercial traveller from Manchester in the 1830s had a great desire to be close to the superstars of his day which led him to an unfortunate mistake. He cultivated a friendship with the local stage manager and so wormed his way backstage on the night that the great William Macready (the Charlton Heston of his day) was acting in Shakespeare's play *Macbeth*. In this way he was able to watch his hero performing from only inches away.

Unfortunately, there was a technical hitch during the murder scene, in which Macbeth leaves the stage, kills the King, and comes back with his hands covered in blood. The stage hand, who was supposed to be waiting in the wings with a bowl of bright red cochineal for Macready to dip his hands in, had got drunk and failed to turn up. In order to save the show, Macready went up to the amazed commercial traveller, hit him very hard on the nose, and smeared the resultant blood onto his hands for the next scene.

The star-struck traveller received a fiver for his pains.

In-Flight Turbulence

On a flight across the United States a potential hijacker suddenly pulled out a revolver on one of the air stewardesses as she went past him.

"Take me to Detroit," he bellowed.

"That happens to be our appointed destination, Sir," she replied politely.

"Oh, OK then," said the gunman, who put his revolver back into his pocket and sat down again.

Just the Man for the Job

A criminal psychopath called Dr R. H. Hales escaped from the Indiana lunatic asylum in which he was being held by stowing himself away in an empty ice-box. When he emerged into the outside world, he immediately applied for the position of Senior Medical Adviser at the Indiana State Prison and, astonishingly, was given the job. "Dr Hales gave a brilliant interview," said a prison spokesperson. "We therefore followed our policy that we did not require references and gave him the job at a salary of $35,000 per annum." The bungle wasn't discovered until Hales was recognised by his new employer from a wanted picture in the local press.

• chapter six •

HOISTED BY YOUR OWN PETARD

*T*his is the classic back-fire kind of mistake – a "petard" being a kind of cannon-shot. Coined by Shakespeare in 'Hamlet', the phrase arises when the hero intercepts a letter which his treacherous schoolfriends, Rosencrantz and Guildenstern, are carrying to the King of England. This letter contains a warrant for Hamlet's own execution and the hero secretly changes it to an order for the execution of the double-crossing friends themselves. The villains are thus destroyed by their own cannon-fire.

Corpse Crop

Frederick Field was a little short of money in 1931 when he happened to read about the strangled body of Norah Upchurch, a thirty-one year old prostitute, which had been found by workmen in a building site on Shaftesbury Avenue. Immediately he confessed to the murder knowing that he could not possibly be convicted of the crime.

He was arrested, taken to court and tried. He was found innocent, which he knew he would be, and he then immediately sold his story of persecution to the *News of the World* who made him a martyr of the British justice system and paid him a fortune. Mr Field couldn't believe his luck.

In 1936, he deserted from the RAF and was, once more, strapped for cash. He looked around for some casual work but then happened to catch a good murder in one of the daily newspapers. Immediately he confessed to the murder of Beatrice Sutton, a rich but dead widow. This time he was so convincing that the jury found him guilty and he was hanged later that year.

Political Wind

Ian Sproat, the Conservative minister, got the wind up about the boundary changes for his marginal constituency of Aberdeen South which included a lot of new non-Tory voters. When the 1983 General Election came up, he moved hell and high water to get himself transferred to a seat which would be easier to win and ended up as the Conservative candidate for the traditional Tory stronghold at Roxburgh and Berwickshire.

When the election came up, boat-jumping Sproat lost his new seat to an unknown Liberal and the Tory who replaced him in "unwinnable Aberdeen" romped home by 3,500 votes.

Petard Luck

Sun Pin was the leader of the Chi State army which formed part of modern day China in AD 241. This army was engaged in a long and terrible war against its dreaded enemy the Wei army, which was led by a ferocious commander called Pang Chuan. Sun Pin knew that the Chi State had a reputation for cowardice and that the Wei people despised it. He also knew that if he did not take a radical course of action then the war might go on indefinitely.

As the sun went down one evening he gave the command to light 100,000 bonfires, the whole way along the front line. The next night he ordered 50,000 fires to be lit. On the third night there were a mere 20,000. Pang Chuan's prejudices about the Chi people were confirmed. He ran around his troops triumphantly declaring that he had always known that the enemy were cowards and now he had substantive proof that four-fifths of them had deserted. That very evening he would chase the remaining few soldiers down the ravine and the tiny number of Wei men who were still around would be easily overcome.

Sun Pin carefully calculated how far Pang Chuan would come. He had a tree stripped of its bark and, upon it, he scratched the words: 'Under this tree shall Pang Chuan die.' As night fell, his top archers were lined up directly in front of the pre-marked tree. A little later, just as Sun Pin had planned, Pang Chuan arrived at the designated tree and noticed that all of its bark was missing. He was intrigued and struck a light in order to read the message which was only dimly visible in the terrible blackness of the night. Immediately his body was riddled with a volley of arrows and his army retreated, leaderless and defeated.

Digging your own grave: The petard hoist proper is a single explosive event. But some of the top petarders have a knack of burrowing deeper and deeper into the tunnel of disaster.

Bird in the Bush

In the early seventies, unstable oil prices made the financial markets extremely volatile. Like many other international dealers, Marc Colombo of the Lugano branch of Lloyds Bank International in Switzerland was keen to make a good impression for himself and a good profit for the bank by riding the fluctuating markets.

In November 1973 Colombo reckoned that the American dollar would fall and that the Swiss Franc would remain strong. He therefore committed his bank to buying $34 million the following January with Swiss Francs which he could buy in November for much less than that.

Unfortunately for Colombo, this was a bad error of judgement since the dollar made an immediate recovery and the promised transaction cost the bank over £1 million.

Undeterred, Colombo set about putting the situation to right. He immediately supported his investment in the dollar with another massive sale of Francs. No sooner had he done so than the dollar nose-dived again and he doubled his losses. At this stage Colombo changed tactics. He began to be nervous about the bank's view of his wheeler dealings and decided to continue trading, but to keep all his transactions out of the bank's official ledgers – just until he recovered his losses, mind. He certainly had every intention of putting every penny back in to the bank's funds. Then he started dealing around in earnest.

When Colombo's dealings finally showed up in the London office of Lloyds in the Summer of 1974 he had committed the bank to forward deals worth £235 million – which was considerably more that the bank's entire operations in Switzerland. There was a feverish attempt by the bank's bigwigs to shore up the debt, which all failed to materialise as profit, and Lloyds' shares tumbled by £20 million as soon as the news was made public.

Amazingly, the people who seem to have come off worst out of all of this shady dealing were the shareholders, since Colombo was given a suspended sentence and a mere £300 fine. Anyone, declared the judge, can make a mistake.

Stewed in Your Own Goose

In hot pursuit of knowledge for the good of mankind, many medical researchers have come to an unfortunate end. On 9 April 1626 Francis Bacon, best known for his work *The Advancement of Knowledge*, was investigating the properties of deep frozen food. One of the experiments he employed during his research was the consumption of one whole goose stuffed

with snow. Although he came up with the valuable information that this is not a good way to preserve goose, the
unfortunate cost to himself was that he caught typhoid and
died.

• chapter seven •

WELL-MEANING BLUNDER

T *hey meant well but it all went horribly wrong. Victims of mistake category No. 7 are gifted gaffers with hearts of gold. They're the Winnie the Poohs of the social world and we think you'll love them. Put a love score for each entrant in the table at the end of this chapter.*

Dining with the Queen

Michael Holroyd, the biographer, was once invited to a state banquet with members of the royal family. He was very well positioned, opposite one particularly distinguished lady member of the clan. She began to demonstrate a great ability to mimic accents.

First she did an incredibly accurate imitation of a Yorkshire accent. Michael Holroyd clapped in admiration. Next she managed an absolutely perfect rendition of an Irish lilt. Mr Holroyd murmured in anticipation. Her powers of mime were truly wonderful. Finally she did a third accent, quite brilliantly, and the biographer had to burst into spontaneous applause. He burst out laughing and congratulated Her Majesty heartily.

Now that one, he commented, was truly superb. An absolutely priceless imitation of an accent. The table fell silent and the lady stared. She had been speaking in her own voice.

Well-Meaning Booby Award for the Entire Nineteenth-Century

In 1861 a Swiss banker named Jecker lent the Mexican Liberal government 619,000 pesos, in order to build a new naval fleet. The liberals were already unpopular since they had attempted to destroy the power of the Church by forcibly selling off its lands and, even worse, establishing a civil ceremony of marriage. The Conservatives were desperate to seize back power when the fleet failed and Jecker received bonds to a value of fifteen million pesos. The liberals had clearly set themselves an impossible task. Worst of all, European invaders had been given a pretext to invade Mexico yet again. And promptly did so.

Britain, France and Spain all acted together to demand the resumption of payments and commenced a joint occupation of the country in 1862. Upon the receipt of satisfactory assurances that Mexico would eventually pay up, the British and the Spanish withdrew. The French however did not. Napoleon III unilaterally decided that it was about time Mexico had an Emperor and, what's more, that the Emperor should be one of his immediate relatives. Convinced that the country was still full of gold and untold treasures and the Mexican Conservatives would be just thrilled with the plan, Napoleon III's troops entered Mexico City in 1862 and told the less than ecstatic Conservatives that Archduke Maximilian of Habsburg, brother of Emperor Francis Joseph, would now be their leader.

Maximilian himself was a cautious man. He did go as far as asking Napoleon if he had been popularly chosen; when Napoleon replied "yes", Maximilian sailed off to Mexico to take up his new job. He was a distinguished-looking, honourable man and he really meant well. His new government was bankrupt and he had absolutely no support from any source. Although economy was essential, he inaugurated his reign by spending vast sums of money on the palace of Chapultepec, an old fortress rising over seven thousand feet above the plain of Mexico City. Maximilian constructed a costly carriage drive and decorated the palace with marble and luxury objects while his officers threatened to desert unless they were paid. The Church was clamouring for restoration of its lands. He wanted to please everybody. He thought he might restore some of the lands and pass the Reform Laws at the same time, then everyone would be happy. Nobody liked him very much and by 1865 he resorted to that fail-safe tactic of passing a law that anyone who set themselves up against the empire could be shot on sight.

Meanwhile back in the real seats of power, the American Civil War had ended and Benito Juarez, former liberal leader of Mexico, and now in hiding in the North, started to receive military and financial backing from the United States. Napoleon III had decided that Mexico was a mistake and was costing France far too much money. On discussing the matter with the US, therefore, he summarily decided to withdraw and immediately did.

Maximilian thought that his people might still love him. He and his family had built imperial homes of great splendour in Mexico and ruled with a splendidly liberal hand and tried to

Michael Mates

please all of the people all of the time. Optimistically, he stayed on when every single one of the French troops had left. He really thought he might still have popular support but he was sadly mistaken. Within a few weeks he was captured and shot.

Photo Finish

A current member of the House of Lords, who doesn't really like to have his name associated with this story, was doing his constituency rounds, one afternoon in Norfolk, whilst he was still a Member of Parliament.

On visiting a particularly strategic fete, he was introduced to a very strange-looking woman named Mrs Carruthers. Mrs Carruthers was a leading member of the local gardening society and claimed to have organised the entire fete. She had enormous teeth and a very long face, and she spent the whole afternoon following the MP around the stalls and inviting people to take pictures of her leaning on his arm.

As the afternoon progressed, the MP and his secretary became more and more amused by the absurdity of this behaviour and wondered what Mrs Carruthers might possibly want with all these pictures. They got their answer a week or so later, when the secretary received a letter from the lady, enclosing a photograph of herself and the MP and asking very politely for his autograph.

As the secretary prepared the photograph for signing, he was struck by the beauty of Mrs Carruthers – she was one of those people who looks very strange in real life but rather striking on film. In fact he was so struck by this that he went back to Mrs Carruthers' letter and scrawled "Horseface" across the bottom of it so that the MP would be in no doubt as to who the letter was from.

At lunch that day, the secretary asked the MP whether he had had time to deal with the request from Mrs Carruthers and what he had thought of the photograph. "I've signed it and sent it off", said the rather hurried MP, "and what a spirited woman that Mrs Carruthers turned out to be. It is rare to find someone so ugly with such striking self-knowledge of their physical defects. I was so impressed by the way she signed off in her letter that I wrote on the photograph, 'It was charming to meet you, my very dear Horseface, let us hope we meet again.'

Michael Mates and the Watch

On 24 June 1993, Michael Mates resigned as Minister of State for Northern Ireland due to an unfortunate error of judgement. He felt sorry for Asil Nadir, a Turkish Cypriot millionaire businessman whose financial empire had collapsed and who was in the process of being investigated by the Serious Fraud Squad for alleged financial misconduct. He felt so sorry for him, indeed, that he sent him a watch bearing the sympathetically worded slogan "don't let the buggers get you down".

Although John Major, the British Prime Minister, told MPs that sending expensive gifts to people charged with criminal wrongdoings was not "a hanging offence", and that Mr Mates had broken no rules, the Minister felt that he ought to resign since he had become an embarrassment to the government. This currently appears to be the offence most likely to cause dismissal amongst modern ministers.

Sex in the Library

On a recent visit to the Ongar public lending library this notice was observed in the *Eastern Gazette*:

> The authorities at Ongar library have received a number of complaints about a card in the index file with an entry which read : SEX: SEE LIBRAR-IAN. This has now been changed. The new entry reads: SEX: FOR SEX ASK AT THE DESK.

A visit to the local Ongar junior school, however, yielded the following misunderstandings of the Lord's Prayer: "Give us this day our day in bed" and "Lead us not into Thames

Station". One child had understood that the wafers given during communion were "Cheesus Christ". Another was gaily chirping along to the sign of the cross "In the name of the Father and of the Son and into the 'ole he goes".

Lovely Psycho-Doc

Dr Oliver Sacks, a very well-known British neurologist, tells of a mistake he once made with a patient who turned up at his surgery in 1975 suffering from a rare memory disease called Korsakov's syndrome. The classic symptoms of this illness involve a total loss of memory caused by the alcoholic destruction of the mammillary bodies. Its more curious manifestation is that more recent memories disappear before older ones. The patient who turned up to see Dr Sacks was called Jimmy and was forty-nine years old. He knew his name and talked at great length about his childhood, his school days and his time in the navy. He could remember the name of every ship on which he had served and every port in which he had been stationed. In discussing his life with Dr Sacks he recounted all his experiences with great enthusiasm but could recall nothing that had taken place in the last thirty years.

When Dr Sacks questioned him about his recent life, it appeared that Jimmy fervently believed that it was still 1945 and that the Allies had just won the war. On testing Jimmy's memory more thoroughly, the Doctor discovered that, although Jimmy was an intelligent and articulate man, he had absolutely no recall of any events that had happened since that date. Jimmy was very good at arithmetical calculations, but he could only do them at lightning speed, otherwise he would forget the figures involved halfway through. Jimmy showed extreme amazement when Dr Sacks held up a photo of the moon, as taken from the surface of the planet. He simply could not accept that it was possible to take such a photograph since in 1945 this would have been unheard of and when Dr Sacks patiently explained that it was a genuine image, Jimmy became very irritable and angry and began to panic. When his brother later came to visit him, Jimmy rejected his guest forcefully, saying that this could not possibly be his brother, since his brother was a young man and the gentleman he saw before him was old enough to be his father.

Dr Sacks was very concerned about the apparently total mental cut-off point in 1945. He thought that there might be a medical reason for this very specific date and attempted to establish what this was. His initial method was to use hypnotism, but this failed since Jimmy's memory loss was so total that he could never remember what the hypnotist had told him to do. A nurse was assigned to give Jimmy constant attention and although he could recognise her between meetings he was convinced that this was because she was a fellow-pupil at high school with him. When other patients addressed her as "sister", he would express great surprise that she had decided to leave school in order to become a nun.

Dr Sacks could not work out why Jimmy could not remember anything past 1945. But he thought it might help to draw it to Jimmy's attention that this was so. He asked Jimmy how old he was and Jimmy instantaneously replied that he was nineteen. Dr Sacks picked up a mirror and asked Jimmy to look and describe what he saw. Naturally he saw a grey-haired, middle-aged man. Jimmy was panic-stricken. He became hysterical and thought he was going mad. Dr Sacks realised that he had made a very bad diagnostic error. He assured Jimmy that everything was OK. The whole incident was simply a terrible mistake.

Love chart for well-meaning boobies

BOOBY	INCIDENT	LOVE SCORE
Emperor Max	Blundering rule of Mexico	
"Horseface" MP	Horseface photo mix-up	
Michael Mates	Watch by post incident	
Ongar Librarian	Sex notice disaster	
Dr Oliver Sacks	Mirror memory mistake	

chapter eight

MISTAKEN IDENTITY

M istake category 8 includes mistaken identifications of all kinds. Pay close attention to the anecdotes and unravel the confusion in our mistaken identity grid at the end of the chapter.

What's in a Name?

About halfway through his period of office as the British Ambassador to Cairo, Sir Miles Lampton was knighted in the New Year's Honours List and, overnight, became Lord Killearn. A little while later he and his wife threw a party to celebrate this auspicious event and invited some of the important people who lived in the country. One of these came up to the new Lord Killearn and, grasping his hand and greeting him warmly, he introduced himself and pointed out that he was so glad to meet the couple at last. It was so pleasant to have them in Cairo and not those Lamptons that used to be in charge and whom everyone disliked so intensely.

Sex with Strangers

One of British law's most notoriously absurd mistakes turned on the fact that in order to be convicted of burglary, the prosecution had to prove that a certain Mr Collins had not just raped the alleged victim but that he had entered her property as a trespasser. The court's 1972 judgement was delivered by Lord Justice Edmund Davies and begins:

> This is about as extraordinary a case as my brethren and I have ever heard. Stephen Collins was convicted on 29 October 1971 of burglary with intent to commit rape and he was sentenced to 21 months' imprisonment . . .
>
> Let me relate the facts . . . At about two o' clock in the early morning of Saturday, 24 July 1971, a young lady of eighteen went to bed at her mother's home in Colchester. She had spent the evening with her boyfriend. She had taken a certain amount of drink . . . She has the habit of sleeping without wearing night apparel in a bed which is very near the lattice-type window of her room . . . At about 3:30 am she awoke and she then saw in the moonlight a vague form crouched in the open window. She was unable to remember, and this is important, whether the form was on the outside of the window sill or on that part of the sill which was inside the room (*this was crucial to the legal case*). The young lady then realised several things: first of all that the form in the window was that of a male; secondly that he was a naked male; and thirdly that he was a naked male with an erect penis. She also saw in the moonlight that his hair was blond. She thereupon leapt to the conclusion that her boyfriend, with whom for some time she had been on terms of regular and frequent sexual intimacy, was paying her an ardent nocturnal visit. (*The law report does not record whether he was in the habit of doing this on a regular basis.*) She promptly sat up in bed, and the man descended from the sill and joined her in bed and they had full sexual intercourse. But there was something about him

which made her think that things were not as they
usually were between her and her boyfriend. The
length of his hair, his voice as they had exchanged
what was described as "love talk" and other features
led her to the conclusion that somehow there was
something different. So she turned on the bedside
light, saw that her companion was not her boyfriend
and slapped the face of the intruder, who was none
other than the appellant (*Collins*). He said to her,
"Give me a good time tonight", and got hold of her
arm, but she bit him and told him to go. She then
went into the bathroom and he promptly vanished.

The alleged victim in the case was absolutely adamant that, had
she known that Collins was not her boyfriend she would not
have had sex with him. There was however no suggestion of
any force being used. The judgement continues :

(Collins) went on to say that he knew the complainant because he had worked around her house. On
this occasion, desiring sexual intercourse . . . he
walked around the house, saw a light in an upstairs
bedroom, and he knew that this was the girl's
bedroom. He found a step ladder, leaned it against
the wall and climbed up and looked into the bedroom. What he could see inside through the wide
open window was a girl who was naked and asleep.
So he descended the ladder and stripped off all his
clothes, with the exception of his socks, because
apparently he took the view that if the girl's mother
entered the bedroom it would be easier to effect a
rapid escape if he had his socks on than if he was in
his bare feet. That is a matter about which we are not
called on to express any view and would in any
event find ourselves unable to express one. Having
undressed, he then climbed the ladder and pulled
himself up on to the window sill. His version of the
matter is that he was pulling himself in when she
awoke. She then got up and knelt on the bed, she put
her arms around his neck and body and she seemed
to pull him into the bed. He went on: "I was rather
dazed, because I didn't think she would want to
know me. We kissed and cuddled for about ten or

fifteen minutes and then I had it away with her but
found it hard because I had had so much to drink"
. . . Now, one feature of the case which remained at
the conclusion of the evidence in great obscurity is
where exactly the appellant was at the moment
when, according to him, the girl manifested that
she was welcoming him. Was he kneeling on the sill
outside the window or was he already inside the
room, having climbed through the window frame,
and kneeling on the inner sill, thereby having
committed the trespass prior to her welcoming
invitation?

Unless the jury were entirely satisfied that the
appellant made an effective and substantial entry
into the bedroom without the complainant doing or
saying anything to cause him to believe that she was
consenting to his entering it, he ought not to be
convicted of the offence charged.

Eventually, after much judicial consideration, it was felt that it
could not be established that any part of Collins' body had
entered the room uninvited before the alleged victim invited
him in herself. Collins, who therefore had his conviction
quashed, must have considered himself a very fortunate
man indeed.

Bad King James

One afternoon King James VI of Scotland, later to become King
James I of England, was out hunting near Perth, when his
friend Alexander Ruthven, a beautiful boy and the brother of
the much-loved Earl of Gowrie, rode up to him and asked him
over for supper in Gowrie's castle nearby. After some hemming
and hawing, the King, who liked the company of beautiful
boys, agreed and Alexander rode off home to make prepara-
tions.

The King duly arrived at Gowrie's castle with a small
company of men and was given a modest supper – due to

the lack of time for preparation. According to some reports the Earl of Gowrie behaved rather strangely at supper and didn't spend as much time talking to the King as he ought to have. The King, at least, was keen to tell everyone that the Earl had behaved strangely.

Just as the meal was ending, young Alexander and the King went off together to an upper room in the castle where – according to the King – Ruthven promised to introduce the King to a Jesuit spy he had caught that afternoon. About half an hour into the enquiry, which, for reasons best known to the King, involved him and Ruthven being locked by themselves in a room containing nothing but a bed, a number of people in the street below the bedroom window heard a loud hullabaloo emanating from the chamber in which they knew the King was conducting a special, private investigation. Worried for their monarch's safety, they quickly alerted the King's soldiers who rushed up to the room and found James and Alexander on their own, apparently wrestling. Alexander was immediately killed by the guards.

The Earl of Gowrie ran to the bedroom to discover his brother dead on the floor. King James immediately claimed that the two men had plotted to kill him and that he had somehow miraculously escaped the effects of treason – well, what else could he say? – and Gowrie too was instantaneously executed.

A huge number of influential people all over Europe didn't believe the King, who immediately started ferreting around for evidence to incriminate the Earl and his brother. Not a single person could be found to give evidence against the young nobles, and there was a storm of protest. According to the brutal custom of the time, the corpses of the brothers were taken to Edinburgh and subjected to the pantomime of a trial. In October (when they had already been dead for ten weeks in mid-summer) the rotting bodies were hanged, drawn and quartered and their heads were stuck on poles above Cowgate in Edinburgh.

None of this prevented James succeeding to the English throne just three years later.

Piltdown Man

In 1913 Charles Dawson, a solicitor and amateur anthropologist, was digging about in a gravel pit in Sussex when he came across the skull fragments and bones of a creature which looked remarkably human. He published his findings in the *Quarterly Journal of the Geological Society of London*, claiming that, at last, here was the incontrovertible evidence for Charles Darwin's theory of evolution – he had discovered the remains of the missing link in the evolutionary chain between ape and man. It was remarkably fortunate for believers in the Empire that the earliest man just happened to be British. The reconstructed skull was named Eoanthropus Dawsoni as a tribute to the man who found it and the whole scientific world was abuzz with the news.

Meanwhile back in Piltdown, the closest village to the site of the gravel pit in which the bones were found, all sorts of things were happening. The town had become a tourist attraction and

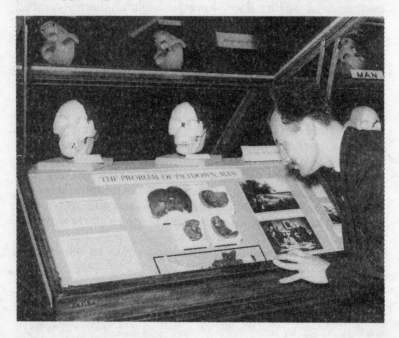

The problems of Piltdown Man

coachloads of eminent scientists were to be seen wandering around the area and checking out the site. Further evidence was found to support the original claim and the bones were given to the British Museum who were just thrilled at their own importance and sent copies of the bones to museums all over the world. Piltdown Man had a place in history.

Years later, when dating techniques had improved beyond recognition, the bones were re-examined and discovered to be not 500,000 years old, as Charles Dawson had believed, but a mere 50,000. Piltdown Man's teeth were twentieth-century and, rather more drastically, not actually human at all but those of an orang-utan.

Maiden Voyage

On 28 November 1720 a court in London was called to pass sentence on a large number of pirates who had all been captured in Jamaica. A certain Lieutenant Barnet testified that he had caught the whole band of brigands by boarding their boat off the north coast of the island and they had all been so unprofessionally drunk that they had all, except two, offered no resistance.

The whole crew were thus hauled to London in chains, the two who had put up a fight being most securely manacled. One of the two had even fired a shot at members of his own crew, enraged at their lack of masculinity in the face of adversity. All the other sailors had conceded defeat meekly, most being incapable of coherent speech.

The death sentence was declared on every single member of the crew and the court went through the ritual of asking if anyone knew of a good reason why this should not be carried out. Normally this question was met with stony silence. On this occasion, however, the two boisterous young lads who had been the only ones to offer resistance called out the age-old expression "Milord, we plead our bellies". This was greeted with hoots of derisory laughter since it was the phrase used by young ladies to indicate that they were pregnant and thus could not be hanged. Everyone in the tribunal naturally considered that this was part of the general ribald exchange for which pirates were notorious and carried on laughing but the sailors would not give up. Eventually a court physician was called in to examine the two young men. He came back to the court to announce to a stunned audience and even more stunned crew that the two young men were, in fact, two young women and both were pregnant. The two women, whose stories are now well-known, were called Ann Bonny and Mary Read and both had succeeded in being mistaken for men over an admirably long period of time.

Ann Bonny was apparently the daughter of a serving maid and a married solicitor, born in the Irish town of Kinsale. The affair between her parents caused such a scandal that the two fled Ireland, her father leaving behind him a wife, two children and a hitherto highly respectable practice.

They set up home in Carolina and within a few years Ann's father had become a wealthy man. Ann's mother died and Ann became a potentially very wealthy and therefore much wooed inheritress. She appears to have been unusually independent for someone of her times. On one occasion an ardent fan received nothing for his flirtatious pains save a good, sound thrashing. Very shortly after this Ann eloped with an apparently unemployed sailor called James Bonny and the two of them went to live on the romantically outlawed colony of New Providence in the Bahamas, which had been set up by the legendary Captain Woodes Rogers.

James Bonny turned out to be such a total waste of space that he was not only a good-for-nothing sailor but an even worse outlaw. He betrayed every pirate he came across to the authorities and thus sustained the intense dislike of everyone on the island but particularly that of his wife.

A proper pirate turned up on the island and immediately captured the romantic imagination of Ann Bonny and she decided to marry him instead. To be fair to the couple, and to Ann's genteel upbringing, they did try to get what was known as a divorce by sale from her first husband. This was a process where, by mutual consent, a wife could be transferred by bill of sale from one man to another. Bonny, true to form, betrayed both of them to the governor of the islands and thus forced the couple to effect a daring escape and head for the open seas. Ann dressed up in seaman's clothes and, together, the pair overpowered the night-watchman at the harbour, stole his boat and set off to sea to join the most notorious boat on the waves, *Haman's Sloop*.

Extraordinarily Rackam was the only man on board who knew that Ann was a woman, even when she, apparently, had to be set ashore in Cuba in order to give birth to their first child.

Ann was clearly a woman of spirit. A little while after the birth of her first child a new sailor appeared on board and Ann was seriously attracted to him. She had to be very careful about revealing her secret but, eventually, no longer being able to control her lovelorn passion, she took the young man aside and declared her undying love. Much to her astonishment, the young man took off his hat to reveal his luscious long tresses – he was a she and she was called Mary Read. Rackam, who had been watching his wife with jealous intensity, leapt out from behind the mainsail in an insane fury and accosted the two women. They therefore had no choice but to share their secret with him. Mary Read's story appears to have been even more complicated than Ann's but she also appeared to have a husband on board, who was even more spineless than Ann's. Mary had apparently already saved her husband from death by fighting a duel on his behalf and winning.

These bizarre anecdotes saved the two women from the gallows and instead they were no doubt thrilled to be sentenced to life. Mary Read died in childbirth in prison but Ann Bonny survived and, apparently, several of her father's former friends turned up to bail her out and took her back to Jamaica where she lived for many years in peaceful retirement.

Mouth-Organ Man

On one occasion the humorous magazine *Punch* received a long and not particularly funny story from Larry Adler, the harmonica player and broadcaster, in New York. They were undergoing a difficult spell financially and considered themselves very fortunate that anyone famous had bothered to send them a piece at all.

The story was not only unfunny but also remarkably badly written. The senior editor spent a great number of man-hours fiddling about with the sentence structure, rewriting the words and changing the grammar and spelling. Eventually the piece

was readable and, breathing a sigh of relief, the editor printed it
proudly in the next issue of his illustrious but failing magazine.

Almost immediately another complete manuscript arrived
from New York. This time the accompanying note was just a
little bit longer than the first had been. "I am so very glad that
you used my first story", proclaimed the writer. Since it had
been so well received he thought that the editorial staff might
like to know a little bit more about him. He was a nineteen year
old student at Columbia University who happened to share a
name with a world-famous harmonica player.

Ghostblaster

It was 1803 and the citizens of Hammersmith were all very
worried. One of the local residents had recently been brutally
murdered and the body had been recovered with the throat
violently slit. They were convinced that the spirit of the
murdered man was roaming along the banks of the River
Thames, a ghost of his former self. Tales abounded of sightings
of the terrifying, white monster with its horns and its howling
shrieks. One woman went out for a walk, caught sight of the
dreaded creature and instantaneously died of fright.

Two locals, Mr Smith, a highly respected customs officer, and
his friend Mr Girdler, the neighbourhood watchman, were
determined to form a vigilante group and rid their streets of
this terrible threat. Mr Thomas Millwood was a bricklayer. On
the evening of 3 January 1804 he went to visit his parents, who
happened to live in Hammersmith, on his way home from work.
By the time he left it was quite late and he was still wearing his
normal work uniform which consisted of long white trousers
and a white shirt. Mr Smith and Mr Girdler were on their night-
watch when they caught sight of a ghostly white spectre ambling
slowly along the banks of the Thames. They immediately
concluded that this must be their prey and challenged the ghost
to fight them. Being a peaceable soul, mistakenly assuming that
he had just encountered two drunken men also on their way
home, Mr Millwood decided to turn the other cheek and,
ignoring their shouts, he walked on. Mr Smith panicked and

shot Mr Millwood who collapsed dead in front of him. Seeing the blood, Mr Smith immediately realised his terrible mistake and surrendered himself to a passing wine merchant.

A mere ten days later he was up in the dock at the Old Bailey accused of murder. Many of the good citizens of Hammersmith came to give evidence about the terrifying reputation of the ghost. Mr Girdler told the jury at great length that Mr Smith was a generous and kind man and one of the best friends he had ever had. Mr Smith himself made a short but moving speech explaining that, whatever he had done, he had done it with the interests of his beloved Hammersmith at heart. The judge, in his summing up, explained to the jury that if they were satisfied that Mr Smith had shot the victim intentionally then he was guilty and there was no defence which could save him. He mistakenly ignored the possibility that Mr Smith might have had the intention to shoot a ghost but certainly not a man. The jury had no choice but to convict. The accused was sentenced immediately to death on the following Monday with his body to be given to surgeons for medical experiments.

Fortunately for Mr Smith a pardon arrived in the nick of time. But the bricklayers of Hammersmith were thereafter very careful always to change into their own clothes before they went home from work.

Ich Bin Ein Berliner

During the Second World War Irving Berlin, the composer, had a massive smash hit with *White Christmas*. It was considered a tremendous morale boost for Allies everywhere. To celebrate he made a short trip to Britain.

One of Winston Churchill's aides noticed that Mr I. Berlin had arrived in the country and pointed out this heartening fact to the Prime Minister, who was rather too busy to follow current trends in popular culture. The aide was thus surprised at the alacrity with which Churchill sprang into the air and positively urged him to invite the great man to a special reception.

Irving Berlin was honoured and flattered to be considered a man of such importance. He was frankly astonished on going

into dinner to be seated right next to the great leader. He was
interested in current affairs but he realised that he was a little
out of his league on this occasion.

Churchill turned to him with a great air of concentration and,
leaning forwards over the soup, he said:

"So tell me, Mr Berlin, how do you think the war is going?"
Irving was thrown. He didn't really feel in a position to
respond; he really wasn't able.

"Come now," said Churchill, "a man of your stature. No
false modesty here. Now tell me, if you were me, what would
your next step be?"

Mr Berlin was silenced. He was at a loss for words. He raced
his way through the remaining courses, desperately hoping
that no-one would notice his presence or ask him for an
analysis of current military matters, about which he knew
no more than the average popular music composer.

After the meal all of the guests departed. Winston Churchill
turned around to his wife and his aide and remarked that the
Berlin fellow was a remarkably thoughtful chap, terribly
natural and unpompous given that he was one of the world's
leading philosophical thinkers. His enthusiasm for his dinner
guest had been fired by the wrong first name – not knowing
anything about white Christmases, he had assumed that I.
Berlin was Isaiah Berlin, the philosopher. Mrs Churchill
thought it was all very amusing.

Knocking Shop

Elizabethan theatres were places of sex and scandal. The actors,
who were always either men or boys, were therefore very keen
to make time for interacting with members of the opposite sex
at any available opportunity. Richard Burbage, who was
Shakespeare's star actor, and generally considered to be a
pretty damn sexy fellow, used to arrange assignations while
he was performing onstage. On one occasion, he managed to
nip out in the interval of *Richard III*, in which he was playing the
king, in order to experience a rendez-vous with a particularly
enthusiastic member of the audience.

Richard, who was naturally in a bit of a hurry, was surprised to find his way barred by an embarrassed servant, furtively guarding the door. The fan, it appeared, was already inside, pursuing her devotion with the Bard himself. Richard was furious at being so humbled and banged on the door loudly. Eventually, Shakespeare who was getting fed up with the interruption, sent down a note which bore the message "William the Conqueror comes before Richard III". The anonymous fan either didn't notice or didn't care.

Art Botch

Dr Abraham Bredius, a Dutch art-historian, was very boastful about his expertise in the seventeenth-century artist, Vermeer. In 1938, he discovered a new painting by his hero called *The Disciples on the Road to Emmaus*, which was immediately bought by the famous Boymans Museum in Rotterdam for the huge sum of £58,000.

Unfortunately, The Disciples was actually the work of Hans van Meegeren, an art student, who had specifically painted the picture to expose Bredius and the art cognoscenti in The Netherlands. Bredius was later taken in by ten other paintings by van Meegeren and the fraud was only discovered when the latter owned up to selling an imitation Vermeer to Goering in 1945 and subsequently confessed all.

Bredius' influence was so powerful that nobody believed van Meegeren until he painted another Vermeer, *Jesus and the Scribes*, under their very noses.

Christopher Columbus

Born in 1451 in the Italian port of Genoa, Christopher Columbus was attracted to water. He went to sea as a pimpled youth,

proceeded to marry the daughter of a Portuguese navigator
and settled down happily in Lisbon.

Christopher was very highly influenced by his reading of a
fashionable book of the period, Ptolemy's *Geography*. From this
work Columbus learnt two main facts: (1) that the world was a
perfect sphere (which is clearly a mistake) and (2) that the
known world extends in a continuous land-mass from the
western extremities of Europe to the easternmost limit of Asia
and that between the two ends of this land-mass on the other
side of the sphere, there was one single intervening ocean
(which was clearly also a mistake). Theoretically, it would
thus be possible, according to Ptolemy, to cross from Europe
to Asia via the Atlantic Ocean.

Ptolemy also reckoned that the proportions of land to ocean
were identical and therefore the Atlantic would be too wide for
any vessel in existence at the time to be able to cross it. Columbus
didn't like this part of the book so he dismissed it as incorrect.

With the assistance of his brother and expert chart-maker,
Bartholomew Columbus, Christopher, a most charming and
sophisticated fellow, used the parts of Ptolemy which sup-
ported his argument, to acquire the support of Ferdinand and
Isabella of Spain in his mission to discover the other route to the
Indies.

On 3 August 1492, Columbus embarked from the port of
Palos in his trusty boat the *Santa Maria* and set sail for a
destination due west. On 12 October 1492, after quelling a
potential mutiny on board by sheer force of personality, he
landed in the Bahamas, believing himself to be in China. He
kept notes on the native people, as if he were making notes
about the Chinese, and he explored Haiti. He returned to
Barcelona to a hero's welcome.

In September 1493, Columbus once again set sail, landing
this time in Puerto Rico which he considered to be an island in
the Indian Ocean. This is when things began to go badly wrong.
A large number of colonisers had sailed with Columbus,
thinking that they were about to get rich on gold. Columbus, however, was very keen that they should all plant
vegetables. The unhappy Spaniards seized most of the boats
and returned to Spain. Those who remained were disgusted to
discover that the local food was horrible, the weather was lousy
and there wasn't a nugget of gold to be found.

Columbus wasn't a man to be easily deterred by the big
things in life. It was during his third voyage to the East Indies

that Magellan and Da Gama actually did reach the Orient, thus discrediting Columbus completely whilst he was still claiming that Honduras was, in fact, Japan. Two years later, he returned to Spain, a broken man, but still pretty wealthy.

Over 'ere Landlord

The eighteenth-century playwright, Oliver Goldsmith, was riding late in Kent one night, when he lost his way and found himself in a town called Ardagh.

It started to rain, so he stopped a passing fencing master named Kelly and asked him where the best house in the town was to be found, intending to spend the night there. Kelly, who assumed, quite reasonably, that he was enquiring about local architecture, directed him to the splendid and ancient residence of Sir Ralph Featherstone, a local landowner. Goldsmith found the house, blustered in out of the cold and promptly ordered himself a hearty supper. Featherstone himself came downstairs to find out what was going on and Goldsmith warmly invited him and his entire family to join him for a meal. The landowner, an old friend of Goldsmith's family but a stranger to Goldsmith himself, recognised the young writer and decided to play along with the charade.

Goldsmith went on to order two bottles of wine, a bed for the night and a hot bowl of porridge for his breakfast before he tried to pay his bill and discovered his error. This incident is said to have inspired his most famous play *She Stoops to Conquer*.

Nixon Likes Jazz

In 1971, the White House threw a birthday party for the band leader Duke Ellington. The great Cab Calloway was one of the guests and he was a bit shy of the grandness of the occasion and so stood quietly waiting his turn in the receiving line. To his surprise, President Nixon strode straight over to him and pumped his hand so warmly that Calloway thought he must be a special fan. "Pat and I love your music," crooned the President, "and it's a great honour to have you here. Happy Birthday, Mr Ellington."

Son of God

Sabbatai Zevi, who was born and brought up in Smyrna, was a Jew who considered, for reasons best known to himself, that he was the Messiah. From 1651 until 1665 he travelled around the large Jewish communities of the Middle East claiming not only that he was the Messiah but also that he would usher in the millennium quite specifically in the year 1666. By 1665 he had convinced a large number of other people of this notion and his disciples spread the word with great enthusiasm to many others.

By the time he returned to his native Smyrna in 1665 he received a hero's welcome. Everyone went mad. All the natives prepared for a speedy exodus to the Holy Land, considering that the Age of the Messiah was about to descend upon them. Businessmen everywhere were so sure of the correctness of their facts that they neglected their trade and began to sell up, in preparation for the imminent return to Jerusalem.

A necessary first step to the Age of the Messiah was that the Sultan of the Ottoman Empire had to be deposed. Following this simple logic, and knowing that they could not fail, Sabbatai and his followers all landed on the Dardanelle Coast early in 1666 and were promptly arrested by local policemen and dragged to Constantinople in chains and pitiful ignominy.

This did not however dampen the ardour of his followers who decided that the fact that he had not been massacred straight away was even clearer proof that he must be the true Messiah. A constant procession of adoring visitors streamed through the prison in Constantinople where Sabbatai played it up no end and continued to disseminate tales of his miraculous endeavours.

Contemporary reports indicate that in large commercial towns all over Europe, where the Jews led the business world, stagnation of trade took a terrible toll on all local enterprise. Citizens everywhere packed up their linen and their dry goods in order to prepare for the imminent journey home.

The Sultan had to think up a sophisticated way of coping with the problem without making Sabbatai into an instant martyr. He thus attempted to convert Sabbatai to Islam. Almost immediately the plan worked. Curiously many of his original followers could not accept Sabbatai's mistake and resolved it in their own minds by continuing to pursue their original conviction with a somewhat muddled vigour. They also converted in their hundreds.

Nazi View

"Christ cannot possibly have been a Jew. I don't have to prove that scientifically. It's a fact!" said Joseph Goebbels.

Bonking in the Bois de Boulogne

Famous men have always held a certain allure for members of the public and, according to contemporary and highly scandalised local newspaper reports, Anatole France, the nineteenth-century French philosopher and novelist, was no exception. On one memorable occasion he was noisily engaged in sexual activity with a somewhat recalcitrant girlfriend in the main Parisian park, the Bois de Boulogne, when an enthusiastic and moustachioed gendarme leapt out from behind one of the other bushes in a state of some agitation.

"Sir", he exclaimed, "your behaviour is reprehensible and, indeed, highly detrimental to the moral conduct of all local children. I beg you and your lady friend to desist immediately or

I shall be forced to arrest you, Sir, with or without your clothes."

France sat upright and drew out from within his jacket pocket a visiting card which he showed to the gendarme, who was immediately contrite.

"Oh Sir, I'm so terribly sorry, Sir, I had no idea that you were a member of the Academie Francaise. Pray forgive me, Sir. I couldn't possibly be expected to guess. All kinds of unsuitable people come to have sex here. Had I known I wouldn't have dreamt of bothering you."

The recalcitrant ladyfriend was thrilled since she had not known that her partner was a celebrity. They went back into the bush and continued to disturb its roots with great vigour.

Mistaken Identity Grid

Character A	Relationship	Character B
A drunken teenage girl	said Happy Birthday to	The son of God
King James I	had sex in the Bois de Boulogne with	The Piltdown Man
Charles Dawson	proclaimed to the world that he was	The East Indies
Anne Bonny & Mary Read	mistook the American subcontinent for	Isaiah Berlin
The editor of Punch	lovingly caressed a naked man in socks called	Anatole France
Mr Smith	thought he had discovered the missing link when he dug up	Sir Miles Lampton
An Elizabethan courtesan	dressed up as	Cab Calloway
Winston Churchill	shot	two effeminate pirates
President Nixon	ordered breakfast from	the Elizabethan actor Dick Burbage
Dr Abraham Bredius	innocently insulted	the beautiful boy Alex Ruthven
Christopher Columbus	locked himself in an upper room with	Hans Vermeer
Oliver Goldsmith	went to bed with Shakespeare thinking he was	Larry Adler
Sabbata Zevi	wanted to have dinner with	an alleged rapist called Mr Collins
A French gendarme	thought he had discovered a new work of art by	a ghost
An ambassadorial guest	thought he was corresponding with the celebrated mouth organist	Sir Ralph Featherstone

• chapter nine •

EVERY DOGMA
HAS ITS DAY

I *deologues are generally fools. They ride their hobby-horses into the*
ground without looking to right or to left of them. They take no
account of external circumstances or practical consequences. If there
are enough of them in one place, this kind of thing happens.

Humble Pi

Pi, as every schoolchild knows to their utter tedium and
ultimate frustration, is an extremely difficult number with
which to do mathematical calculations. It is also an extremely important one. Its value, for general purposes, is taken
to be 3.142 although, in fact, it is an endlessly recurring
number. Its value, for specific purposes, is that it represents
the ratio of the circumference of a circle to its diameter (is
that right?).

This was all too complicated for the General Assembly of
Indiana who passed a law in 1897 declaring that they weren't
going to put up with any of that frivolous nonsense after the
decimal point and they were going straight for the concrete
figures. The law stated that, in the area of Indiana only, pi

would be worth a solid 4. As a consequence every single clock in the State gained roughly fifteen minutes an hour.

Yet More Messianic Truths

The crazy evangelist, William Miller, founded his own cult in the 1820s and persuaded all the members of it that the world would end in 1833. There are apparently an awful lot of people out there waiting for the news that the universe is on the brink of destruction, since he, too, rapidly gained a large and ardent following. When 1833 didn't work, he tried 1834. When that didn't work either, he bought himself an entire decade and settled for sure for 1843. That didn't work either. Now pursued by thousands of followers all over the United States, he decided he couldn't disappoint them and gave it one last try with 1844 and then gave up entirely.

His followers were not so easily deterred. Many joined the Seventh Day Adventists.

Vietnam War (Likewise Korea, Afghanistan etc.)

Following the Geneva Conference of 1954, Vietnam was divided into North and South. In October 1961 President Kennedy sent General Maxwell Taylor to discuss with President Ngo Dinh Diem the perceived threat of the spread of Communism throughout south-east Asia. In February 1962 Military Assistance Command was created to prevent this and US military aid began in earnest.

By 1965 the US presence in South Vietnam was a more or less permanent fixture. January of that year was a period of intense Communist activity throughout South Vietnam as the Viet

Cong and North Vietnamese forces launched assaults on military targets and cities throughout the country and thus caused enormous numbers of casualties, mostly amongst South Vietnamese troops. The Northern forces temporarily succeeded in cutting South Vietnam in two by carrying out a massive thrust from the highlands and down to the coast.

In early February the Viet Cong forces attacked a US installation and this gave President Johnson, who had by this stage automatically succeeded the assassinated JFK and was altogether much keener on the whole project than his predecessor had been, the much needed opportunity he had been waiting for. He ordered the South Vietnamese and US army and navy to begin systematically bombing a succession of selected military targets.

On 8 March, the US Marine Brigade landed at Danang and immediately went into action to repel an army that had been supported quite independently by both China and the USSR. The US in this way entered what was to become the longest, messiest and most unpopular war in its history.

There was no fixed front and there were guerrillas everywhere. The enemy was led by General Vo Nguyen Giap who had already commanded his troops against the French army and had thus perfected the art of guerrilla warfare a long time before the US army had grasped what it was. In the whole war, American ground forces never actually managed to gain an inch of territory from the North Vietnamese forces and there was never a single conventional battle in the traditional military meaning of the word. All of these problems were aggravated by the fact that the whole endeavour was being watched daily, for the first time in the history of a war, in every US living room on the television. This was a disaster as far as public opinion was concerned. Civilian frustration was added to by the fact that although they could watch their troops being horribly decimated before their own eyes, military leaders persisted in maintaining an over-optimistic line, which the people knew could not be true.

Despite the rapid commitment of seven additional US grand battalions and the commencement of raids on Communist bases in South Vietnam, the war remained in stalemate. In 1966 the US launched its first prolonged offensive which comprised long, continuous launches across areas of the country rather than the short, sharp raids they had hitherto been pursuing. These were no more successful than the raids had

been, with the guerrillas merely disappearing into jungle areas
into which the troops could not follow. In 1967 two massive
offensives were launched, Cedar Falls and Junction City.
Although the offensives were successful in splitting the Communist forces, these merely regrouped in more entrenched
positions along the borders of Laos and Cambodia which, in
turn, led to the Communist-led Tet offensive of 1968. Tet was a
tactical defeat for the Communists who suffered major casualties and gained no ground but, much more importantly, it was
a terrible blow to US public opinion since it happened just at a
time when military leaders there had assured the public that
the Communists would imminently collapse. The US public no
longer had any faith in their military strategists or in the war
and given that by 1969 the US presence had increased in
numbers to 543,482 troops, this was a political disaster.

Alongside the fact that the troops sustained 8,500 casualties,
enormous side problems arose. Certain South Vietnamese
clubbed together with corrupt US soldiers to create black
markets, to rob from munitions dumps and to make as much

John de Lorean sits in one of his De Lorean sports cars

money as possible out of stealing from the military camps. Drug abuse boomed amongst the disillusioned troops and seven out of every ten US soldiers suffered from VD.

The US was now onto its third president. Nixon was very keen to finish the fighting as soon as possible. He ordered US troops to cut off the enemy's military supplies by bombing their suppliers in neighbouring Cambodia. Although vast amounts of hardware were seized, still the supplies continued coming and antiwar feeling, which had rocketed due to this invasion of a hitherto uninvolved country, reached an all-time high. The US government never recovered from this blow, unable to convince its citizens that Cambodia had already been involved. Tens of thousands of Americans deserted, went underground or simply went to jail in order to avoid being killed for a cause in which they had no faith. Meanwhile American POWs remained in limbo since the Communist forces refused to negotiate.

By 1972 General Abram's US forces had virtually succeeded in all of their military aims, drastically curtailing Viet Cong activities and inflicting terrible casualties on the Communists. Ironically, it was all too late. By the time victory had been more or less achieved, the Vietnam War was universally considered to be the worst mistake of the American military ever.

Opera in the Amazon

At the tail end of the nineteenth century there was suddenly a boom in the rubber trade, which focused on the hitherto obscure Brazilian jungle town of Manaus. This outpost of the Amazonian rain forest, quite suddenly, became one of the architectural centres of the world and its new acquisitions included street lighting, South America's very first electric tram system and a very advanced sewage system.

But still the new millionaires of the South had not managed to spend their money and so they decided to build the world's finest opera house, which would be called the Teatro Amazonas. Completed in 1896, this magnificent auditorium proudly boasted a dome of golden tiles, elaborate murals and the finest acoustics.

This feat of architecture was, unfortunately, lost on the very
sparse local population, most of whom were rubber workers and
very few of whom had ever heard an opera, let alone seen one.
The entire local catchment area consisted of 35,000 people and the
opera house could seat almost a tenth of those in one go. Almost
immediately the building was deserted and its prize possession, a
giant chandelier, came symbolically crashing to the floor.

Nowadays there is no significant rubber industry in Manaus
and the building is used as a practise room by the local school
choir, six times a year.

Tall Storeys

During the 1980s Michael Heseltine and Geoffrey Howe
dreamt up the worst conceived experiment in urban regeneration ever to hit the heavens of East London. The sadly
underused, architecturally decrepit Docklands, they thought,
could be transformed by the sole funding of the private sector.
Putting political ideology before practicality was a mistake to
which Mrs Thatcher often fell victim. Olympia & York was the
Prime Minister's idea of a really great firm. The largest
property company in the world, totally privately owned
and a family firm to boot. She was beside herself with
excitement at the prospect of committing a massive package
of public investment to improving transport to the Docklands
in order to assist the cutting edge of private enterprise. Cheap
land and Enterprise Zone tax breaks made Canary Wharf one
of the most heavily subsidised urban regeneration projects in
Europe.

The whole project was to be dominated by the Canary Wharf
tower. Designed by Cesar Pelli, this has now become the tallest
phallic symbol in Europe and the world's single largest office
building. There's just one snag. There's no-one to fill the offices.
Even with expenditure on the part of the Department of
Environment currently standing at some £1.7 billion, there's
still no decent way to get to Canary Wharf. And, even if you
ever manage to get there (which given the current state of the
Docklands Light Railway and the non-existent road system is

extremely rare), no-one thought to provide things for you to do when you get there. So as soon as you can (which is generally not soon since the broken down train on which you arrived has not yet been fixed), you will go home again.

To add to these infra-structural problems, Canary Wharf couldn't have arrived at a worse time financially. The value of UK office space fell by 20% during 1992. To the already existing 40 million empty square feet of office space in London, Docklands has added another 12 million. 40% of its floor area is unlet. Olympia & York, which had agreed to contribute to the Jubilee line underground extension which would service the area, is now not so keen on the project and the character of Docklands, which was originally dubbed "Wall Street on the Water" has sadly never come anywhere close to its name. Most top managers (indeed most middle managers and most lowly managers) refuse to work there. At the current take-up rate, another five years of office space supply remains.

British Industry

John De Lorean was born in 1925 in Detroit, Michigan. On being made redundant from General Motors in Detroit, Mr De Lorean decided to realise his biggest dream – a sports car called the DMC-12. It would have two seats, gull-wing doors and an all-round safety first theme. Revolutionary new plastic processes would be used and John De Lorean began to look for the ideal location for a factory in which to construct his car and in which to award himself a salary of $125,000 a year, and that was in 1976.

Northern Ireland was, at that time, the poorest part of the United Kingdom with an unemployment rate of 50%. Roy Mason, Secretary of State for Northern Ireland at the time, declared his policy to be "Jobs, homes and hope – that's the way to beat the IRA". On 3 August 1978, Northern Ireland and De Lorean signed a risky deal which would create 800 jobs. The risk, in this instance, was being undertaken entirely by the British government who had lent John De Lorean £54 million in grants. This figure was shortly to rise to £84 million.

Problems began almost immediately. Design faults meant that the car was becoming increasingly heavy and might fail safety standard tests. Because of the weight, fuel economy was creeping down. De Lorean declared he would make all the extras, that make a luxury car into a luxury item, optional. Public opinion declared that nobody who could afford to buy a luxury car would buy one without them. Everybody, including the workers in the factory, was losing heart. The factory ran out of money in 1980. The launch was postponed to February 1981.

On 3 December 1980, the very first DMC-12 did actually come off the production line, but a large number of its parts had to be bolted together to make them fit.

John De Lorean was beginning to get desperate and did the first thing that springs into the mind of every boss in dire straits – he fired his private secretary. This was a mistake. Marion Gibson, the lady in question, immediately denounced his more dubious financial dealings to a number of British MPs. Meanwhile, back in Northern Ireland, things weren't going too well with the upmarket design features. In a car museum in Cleveland, a young admirer pulled down the gull-wing doors in order to admire them from the inside, only to discover that they were impossible to reopen. He had to be rescued by the local fire-brigade. There were problems with almost every single car sold, culminating in total recall in November 1981, when the front suspension nuts began to unscrew themselves, as did the De Lorean empire.

Production shut down in May. In October of the same year John De Lorean was arrested for drug-running. The DMC-12 instantly became a collector's item.

Equal Rights for Men and Girls

In 1976 it was politely drawn to the attention of the Irish government that it had not yet complied with the new EEC legislation on equal opportunities for men and women.

Immediately the parliament in Dublin sprang into action and advertised for applicants for a brand new post – that of equal pay enforcement officer. The text came complete with information on the new post's rates of pay – there was one for men and a lower one for women.

chapter ten

FOOT IN MOUTH

M istake category 10. According to the theories of Sigmund Freud, some memories and desires are not available to the consciousness. These impulses are repressed and remain in the unconscious mind, exploding into the conscious mind in indirect and disguised form. Freudian slips need not only be to do with sex.

Some of the mistakes in this chapter, however, are not Freudian slips at all. They're verbal cock-ups caused by inaccuracy, stupidity or ignorance. Sam Goldwyn, the film mogul, was very well-known for his verbal mistakes. On one occasion he was considering making a film about Jesus and the Last Supper. He felt it needed a bit of extra something and that the cast just wasn't quite spectacular enough. "Why only twelve disciples?" he enquired, "Go out and get thousands."

He was also heard to say that "a verbal contract isn't worth the paper it's written on" and on one memorable afternoon, he commissioned an up-and-coming sculptor to create a piece for him with the words "I want you to make a bust of my wife's hands." On another occasion a number of the crew on a particular film set had all been involved in a rather trying dispute. In attempting to placate as many of the argumentative technical staff as possible, Goldwyn stood up to make a pacifying speech which began "We have all passed a lot of water since last week."

Other verbal mistakes for which he was famed included :
"Why did you name your baby Arthur? Every Tom, Dick and Harry is called Arthur."
"Let's have some new clichés."
"A bachelor's life is no life for a single man" and, my particular favourite:
"Anybody who goes to see a psychiatrist ought to have his head examined."

Churchill's Finest Ooh-Er

In 1954 Winston Churchill paid a visit to the engineering plant at Harwell and, on arrival, was taken on an extensive tour of the machine works. He stopped from time to time as he walked around and chatted to the scientists, asking them politely about their work. The first scientist replied, "I make heavy water into uranium," and Churchill nodded politely. He went up to a second scientist and asked him, in turn, what it was that he did. "I make light water to make uranium," replied the technician. Churchill thought about this for a moment and then replied, "I want to make ordinary water but I can't find the urinium."

Whose Turn on Top?

Mrs Margaret Friend, aged forty-eight, of Southend on Sea was arrested and brought to the local magistrates court on a charge of prostitution. She was outraged and, in a spirit of judicial enquiry, the court asked her to assist them by explaining why it was, exactly, that the charge could not possibly be correct.
"Oh," she exclaimed, "there's no way I could ever be a prostitute. I'm far too short-sighted. I'm blind in one eye and only have partial vision in the other. In fact, I can only ever see anyone if they're right on top of me."

Phallic Charm

On the occasion of General De Gaulle's retirement, the French leader decided to celebrate by inviting a large number of political dignitaries and their spouses to lunch. Amongst the many illustrious world leaders present at the table were Dorothy and Harold Macmillan.

Dorothy talked at great length about the remarkable contribution that De Gaulle had made to French history and then, turning to his wife, asked Mrs De Gaulle what she was most looking forward to, now that she had a little more time on her hands.

Mrs De Gaulle beamed away at Mrs Macmillan and, with everyone at the table silent and expectant, she opened her mouth to reply with the words :

"What I most look forward to now is a penis."

U.S. Film Chief Samuel Goldwyn

There was a stunned silence around the table, whilst some of the primmer guests shuffled around on their seats, blushing and embarrassed. General De Gaulle himself rapidly intervened, explaining carefully to his wife that the word was not pronounced in quite that way. She had not been looking forward to 'a penis' but, in fact, to ''appiness'.

Coming Up for Air

"I have just learned that we do have the film of the astronauts' breakfast, which should be coming up shortly" (Frank McGee – BBC News)

In the heat of the moment many's the sporting broadcaster who's simply got carried away by the scent of victory.

"Former Wimbledon Champion Martina Navratilova had a surprisingly easy victory over Andrea Jaegar in the final of the Avon Tournament in Seattle today. She won in straight sex." (BBC News)

"Well the streakers are at it again, this time at a local football game just outside of Boston. I can't figure out this type of behaviour – I guess they just want to show us they're nuts." (Larry Glick of WBZ News, Boston, Massachusetts)

Royal bricks

Lord Portarlingon was invited to an important political occasion at which he walked straight into Queen Victoria. Jumping backwards, in a rather surprised way, the lord recovered himself and looking up at her was heard to say "Damn it Ma'am, I know your face but I cannot put a name to it."

Funny-faced comedian Stephen Fry came up with some splendid royal bricks on the TV Show *Whose Line is it Anyway?* Fry was asked to think of things that you shouldn't say when you meet the Queen. His first response was the amazing line "Whop some skull on that, bitch" – delivered almost too fast for the audience to hear. After delivering the fateful words, Fry was plunged into embarrassment and apology and came up with a surreal follow-up gag. "Oh that reminds me," said Fry to the imaginary monarch, "I must buy a stamp."

Death Wish

"This is a great day for France."
(Richard Nixon in 1974 at the funeral of President Georges Pompidou)

Muddle East

In December 1975 President Gerald Ford drank the health of Anwar Sadat, the leader of Egypt, toasting loudly to "the President of Israel".

Back Pedalling

"I just wanna say," said Mayor Richard Daley of Chicago at a fun-pedal convention for married couple cyclists, "you husbands and wives, if you wanna get along together, you gotta get one of them tantrum bicycles."

Socialite's Cramp?

Laura Corrigan, a famous jet-setter of international repute, amazed her friends by her splendid malapropism after having been to the doctor for indigestive problems. "My doctor told me," she said, "if you want to avoid indigestion, you must masturbate, masturbate, masturbate."

Oral Sex

A current member of parliament tells this story of his early love life, which he, presumably, now regrets:

"When I was an undergraduate, I developed a consuming passion for a very pretty Welsh woman called Myfanwy Lewis. Myfanwy had a lot of admirers and the only way I could get close to her was by swearing blind that I had no sexual interest in her at all, which I did at every opportunity. Eventually, we became friends and I began to ponder what my next move should be.

"Towards the summer, when love was in the air, and we knew each other quite well, I invited Myfanwy around for dinner with two friends of mine called David and Harriet who were very much a couple. The evening passed off pretty well and after the meal we were all a bit tipsy and having a good deal of fun. Then, as spirits rose, David and Myfanwy suddenly got into a terrible drunken row which became more and more heated. Within seconds, David had screamed abuse and left, taking Harriet with him and leaving Myfanwy on my sofa in floods of tears. I went over and hugged her as she clung to me for dear life and bawled her eyes out.

"This was almost more than I could bear and it was everything I could do to offer the reassurances that were required without exploding. After fifteen minutes or so, in which I considered I was putting on a pretty good show, Myfanwy suddenly pulled out the rug from under my feet by shouting 'It's no good. It's no good. You're pretending to be nice. But all you really want to do is to sleep with me.'

"I thought about this one pretty hard and planned my response carefully. 'Myfanwy, Myfanwy,' I claimed resolutely, revelling in the mere sound of her magical name, 'the thought of kissing you had not even entered my mind.' But it didn't come out like that. Instead, the fateful words were uttered: 'Myfanwy Myfanwy. The thought of kissing you had not even entered my mouth.'"

chapter eleven

INATTENTION TO DETAIL (OR BUMBUMS)

F atal flaws of all kinds crop up under mistake category 11, the "Bumbum". Perfect crimes, elegant designs, crisp interrogations – all ruined by a single tiny but crucial oversight.

Mr Bumbum

In one of the London County Courts a barrister, who appeared to be rather tense and nervous, called his first witness into the box. After the witness had sworn the oath, the barrister went through the normal court procedure of asking him to verify his name and address.

"Is it correct", he said, "that your name is Mr Bumbum Fricks?"

"Why no!" exclaimed the irate witness, who was considerably put out by this violent insult to his person, "My name is Mr Bumbum and I am a Fellow of the Royal Institute of Chartered Surveyors."

H owever big or small the plot or plan, just when you thought you had everything covered out jumps Mr Bumbum.

Pearls Before Bumbum

In Preston Crown Court in November 1983 a man accused of the theft of a large amount of jewellery was in mid-trial. His defence was mistaken identity. He wasn't there, didn't know anything about it and it wasn't him. As the Prosecuting Counsel, Peter Oppenshaw, began his cross-examination of the defendant, a large commotion was heard at the back of the courtroom. The defendant's wife had just walked in with several of her friends.

Suddenly one of the victims of the burglary began to shriek hysterically. The wife of the accused had turned up at court wearing most of the victim's family heirlooms. Mr Oppenshaw turned slowly to the jury and, savouring the moment for all it was worth, he declared:

"Ladies and gentlemen, I am sure you will agree that this turn of events has given the accused's line of defence something of a hollow ring."

Bumbum in Rome

Miss Fiona Gordon, nine years old, went on an educational trip to her local museum in County Durham in 1971. Here she came across one of the star exhibits of the collection: a coin labelled very carefully with the notation "Roman AD 135".

Miss Gordon, a remarkably primary school student, immediately pointed out to one of the museum attendants that the labelling on the coin was, in fact, almost 2,000 years out. She recognised the object straight away, she said, as the kind of plastic token that was supplied as a free gift when you collected a certain number of the requisite bottle labels. She had known instantaneously that this was the case since the supplier's distinctive logo was printed on the exhibit.

A curator at the museum explained that labelling difficulties had arisen because the logo consisted of a rather individual capital *R*, which the scientific team had considered to stand for

"Made in Rome", when really it meant "Robinson's", the lemon barley people.

Bumbum in Wax

A dummy hanging by a noose at the Long Beach Amusement Park in California formed part of a "fun house" exhibit in the centre for over five years.

It was such a convincing piece that it was often used as a prop for films which were being shot in the Park. During the filming of an episode of *The Six Million Dollar Man*, one of the film cameramen became dissatisfied with the way in which the right arm was hanging from the body of the dummy and was attempting to adjust it in order to make it look real when the whole arm fell off. On closer examination a protruding bone was noted and he identified the dummy as a human corpse.

Authorities described the corpse as an elderly man of five-foot-three but could not tell when he had actually died. The figure, wrapped in gauze and sprayed with fluorescent paint, had been bought by the amusement park from a local wax museum.

Bumbum on the Side

Anthony Daniels of Enfield in North London thought that his career was made when he gained control of a take-away food outlet in the centre of London. He took control of every aspect of his new business – staff, fresh produce, attractive decor – but one small oversight led to humiliation.

One April evening in 1993 Ms Pothecary, a suitably named nurse, visited "Anthony's Take-away" in the West End and purchased a salad which she carried home and ate. She was chewing through the final morsel when her jaws came to rest against what she believed to be a lump of poorly shredded cabbage. It resisted her attempts to ingest it and so she spat it out and had a quick look. She realised almost immediately that it was the top of someone's thumb complete with thumbnail still intact.

Ms Pothecary put the thumb in the fridge overnight and the next morning marched down to the Camden Environmental Health Department, bearing the digit angrily before her.

Two days later, an official from the council went to investigate at "Anthony's" and found Mr Campos, the cook, busy chopping away, his right hand swathed in bandages. Anthony Daniels was called to the scene. Mr Campos had been shredding cabbage, he explained on behalf of his employee, when he cut off half his thumb and was rushed to hospital. Another employee finished making up the salads but Mr Daniels completely forgot that one crucial detail – the whereabouts of the missing digit.

Mr Daniels, who blamed this mistake on the stupidity of his colleagues, was fined £200. Ms Pothecary was awarded an extra £200 for shock to the system.

Death by Bumbum

In 1906 an excellent chemical called sulfanilamide was discovered which was most efficacious in the treatment of blood poisoning. One US drug company named Massengill cashed in on the discovery by launching a pink raspberry-flavoured medicine called "Elixir of Sulfanilamide". It sold like hot cakes. Unfortunately they decided to dissolve the magical chemical in the deadly poison diethylene glycol and at least 107 people died of kidney failure after taking it. The chemist who had developed the drug died too, from suicide.

Lazy Git (Brother of Bumbum)

A New York bank computer programmer realised in 1970 that if he stole a few cents each month from all the customers in his bank he would become very rich without anyone noticing. In order to do this, he wrote a programme that rounded everyone's balance down to the nearest ten cents each month and transferred the balance into the account of whichever name was last in the alphabetical list of account holders. He then opened an account for himself in the name of A. Zyglit (an anagram of Lazy Git) and settled down happily to become a millionaire.

Things went wrong for the fraudster when a Polish immigrant named Zyzov moved into the neighbourhood and opened an account at the same bank. After a couple of months he politely wrote to the bank to ask why they appeared to be paying such enormous interest on his very small savings. The whole sham was discovered and the programmer was sent down for a number of years. If only he had called himself Zyzyzyk.

Bumbum Abroad

The most famous of all inefficient phrase books is the English–Portuguese one devised by the inimitable Pedro Carolino, who in 1883 created *The New Guide of the Conversation in Portuguese and English*. Mr Carolino, who had little, if any, grasp of our native tongue, was suitably ill-equipped for the linguistic task he had so bravely set himself. Armed only with a Portuguese–French dictionary and a French–English dictionary he set about his guide to the English language by cross-referencing the two, not wishing to confuse matters by testing out the results on any English speakers. This intriguing methodology led to the kind of marvellously spontaneous sounding language he employs in his opening sentences :

"We expect then, who the little book (for the care what we wrote him, and for her typographical correction) that may be worth the acceptation of the studious persons, and expecially of the youth, at which we dedicate him particularly."

This intriguing introduction is followed by a section entitled "Familiar Phrases" which includes such topical tips as "Have you say that?", "Exculpate me by your brother's", "These apricots and these peaches make me to come water in mouth" and that particularly familiar phrase "He laughs at my nose, he jest by me". This chapter is concluded with the words "End First Part's to be followed by familiar dialogues". These, too, are particularly useful. You could greet your new English friends with the words "For to wish the good morning" and you could leave them with the parting shot "Adieu my dear. I leave you. If can to see you at six clock to the hotel, we swill dive together willingly". Helpfully, he offers some good words of advice for exchanging with your local barber:

"Comb me quick; don't put so much pomatum. What news tell me ? All hairs dresser are newsmonger."

He continues with a section entitled aptly "Idiotisms and Proverbs" and these include all of your regulars: "He sin in troubled water", "To look for a needle in a hay bundle" not to forget that old chestnut "It want to beat the iron during it is hot".

Finally, Carolino offers some chatty little anecdotes with which to entertain new friends:

"One eyed was laied against a man which had good eyes that he saw better than him. The party was accepted. I had gain, over said the one eyed; why I se you two eyes, and you not look me who one".

Carolino considered that this phrase was guaranteed to give any London girl on the look-out for a hot night on the town something to reckon with. And who can blame him?

Judge Bumbum

During the 1820s Mr Justice Graham was famed as the politest judge at the Old Bailey. He was extremely courteous at all times. On one occasion sixteen defendants appeared before him accused of petty theft. Mistakenly Mr Graham read out only fifteen of the sixteen names on the indictment before him and sentenced every single one of the fifteen to death. Glumly, the fifteen men trod their weary way back to the cell in which they would await the gallows.

The sixteenth man, whose name had been left off the death list, breathed a sigh of enormous relief. The Clerk of the Court caught sight of him and turned to address the judge. What was to be done with the man whom he had quite mistakenly saved? Mr Justice Graham politely enquired after the gentleman's name and was told by his Clerk that it was John Robins.

"Oh Mr Robins," said the judge in his most deferential way, "I am terribly sorry for the inconvenience I have caused you. I find that I have quite by accident left your name from the list of people doomed to death. It was quite accidental I assure you and I beg your pardon for my mistake. I am truly sorry and can only add to my profound apologies the fact that you will be hanged tomorrow with the rest of them."

Pigott's Bumbum

In 1887 *The Times* published a series of articles which were intended to show that Charles Parnell, the leading Irish nationalist, was an extremely dangerous political agitator. One of the main pieces of evidence used to back up this claim was a letter, supposedly written by Parnell himself, which expressed total support for the murder of the English under-secretary of Ireland by a Republican terrorist. Parnell immediately made a public statement to the effect that the letter was a forgery and, indeed, that he even knew the identity of the forger, one Richard Pigott.

Pigott was charged and Parnell was represented by the leading barrister of his day, Sir Charles Russell. Russell had looked through all of the apparently forged letters very thoroughly indeed. He had paid particular attention to any idiosyncratic spelling mistakes, the most notable of which was the misspelling of the word "hesitancy".

The first few days of the trial had gone very well for Pigott and he had not made a single mistake. Two days into cross-examination Pigott was blooming with over-confidence, which Russell, an experienced observer of men, could tell immediately. Russell had a piece of paper handed up to Pigott and asked him to write some words down on it, inferring that the whole purpose was to have examples of Pigott's handwriting. First Pigott spelt out the word "livelihood" as requested. Then he was asked to write the word "likelihood". A little later Pigott was asked to sign his name and then, finally, almost as an afterthought, Russell mentioned the word "hesitancy". Things were going swimmingly and Pigott was only too happy to oblige. He picked up the pen and immediately and mistakenly wrote the word "hesitency". He was doomed. By the following morning he had fled to Paris where he wrote a signed confession and, within the month, he had shot himself dead.

Bumbum in Space

On 28 July 1962 the Mariner I space probe was launched from Cape Canaveral headed directly for Venus. Never before had this been attempted in so technical a way. The craft would cruise at over 25,000 miles an hour and in only 100 days Mariner would be circling the great planet with the mysterious cloudy rings.

A mere four minutes after take-off Mariner I hurled headlong downwards and straight into the Atlantic Ocean. A subsequent inquiry revealed that the cause of this accident was the absence of a minus sign which had, unfortunately, been omitted from the computer programme. This oversight was a result of human error and cost NASA a staggering £4,280,000.

Armed Bumbums

One dull afternoon in Reno in 1983, Eddie Blake decided to have a go at robbing a bank. "This is a hold-up," declared the note that he handed to the woman behind the counter, "put all the money into a bag and hand it over." Within seconds he was clutching the loot and running for it.

By the time he got home, the police were waiting outside his door to arrest him. He had scrawled the demand note on the back of one of his business cards. It contained his name, address and telephone number.

Clive Castro of Cooperville, Texas, did manage to get safely out of the bank that he had just robbed. He dived into the nearest passenger car, shouting "Drive off buster and make it snappy." The driver made it very snappy indeed. Castro had run into a patrol car which drove him straight to the nearest police station.

Sister Bumbum

Javiar Ortiz, aged twenty-five, of Badajoz, Spain was a higher grade of criminal altogether. For one thing, he realised that the last place to go after a bank raid was home. For sophisticated technical reasons which are not entirely clear to the non-criminal mind, he decided that it would be a great idea to run into the nearest convent and dress up as a nun.

His first mistake was that he became hungry and stole down to the kitchen where he stole a leg of ham which he stuck up his habit. The Mother Superior walked past at this moment and was fairly sure that her convent did not contain any pregnant nuns. His second mistake was that although he was wearing full religious regalia he had not bothered to change out of his size ten Wellington boots. This convinced the Mother Superior of his fake identity. She blew her whistle and twenty eager nuns suddenly surrounded him, separated him from his unsightly habit and turned him over to an astonished local police force.

For Bumbum or for Worse

For over a quarter of a century John Bratby, the painter, was married to a lady called Jean Cooke. Eventually the pair got divorced and some time after that Bratby got remarried to another lady who was called Patricia.

At the registry office, the registrar reached the point in the ceremony at which the ring was required. Patricia turned around to Bratby and asked him to ask the best man for the ring. Following years of domestic ritual Bratby replied, without a moment's hesitation.

"Yes of course Jean."

Dental Bumbum

John Haigh taunted police in London with the idea that he had murdered a rich widow called Mrs Olive Durand-Deacon. When they came to arrest him, he laughed and declared that he had destroyed the body with acid and that, although they would find the sludge in the garden of her house, every trace of identification would now have disappeared.

The police sent a pathologist called Keith Simpson to dig about in the bushes. First he found a gallstone and then, even worse, Mrs Durand-Deacon's acrylic dentures. John Haigh was hanged at Wandsworth prison on 10 August 1949. If he had waited three more weeks to boast about his success, the disintegration of the body would have been complete.

chapter twelve

HOPELESSLY OUT OF TOUCH

J udges are specialists at mistake category 12. The judge who said "And who is Gazza?", the MP who asked "What is E?" and the judge who asked "Who are the Rolling Stones?" seem to have wandered into the twentieth-century by mistake.

Other out-of-touchers just didn't have the slightest idea what was going on around them, whichever century they were born in.

Latin Lover

An Irish labourer was being cross-examined in a very serious case at the Old Bailey and the judge was beginning to get irritated by the line of questioning that the barrister insisted on pursuing. After some time the judge finally interrupted the barrister and asked him in a highly aggravated tone of voice "Has your client never heard of the well-established doctrine *'quamdiu se bene gesserit'*?" to which the barrister immediately replied "With great respect, my Lord, when the boys gather on a Saturday night on the bogs of Ireland they talk of nothing else."

Safe as Houses

During the American Civil War, General John Sedgwick rode to
examine the position of his troops, stationed as they were, in
May 1864, on an elevation in the State of Virginia. The men
were a little jumpy since they had all been warned about the
incredible firing power of the Confederate troops. Sedgwick
laughed at them for their innocence and assured them that
there was really nothing to worry about. The Confederates, he
said, couldn't hit an elephant at this distance. He was immediately shot dead by a bullet straight in the brain.

Daft 'Ap'orth

In 1925 an American tourist name Sean Lansdowne made the
mistake of buying Nelson's Column for £6,000. The salesman
was none other than the well-known Scottish fraudster, Arthur
Ferguson.

Boil-Sufferers Beware

Boil-sufferers beware. Many sick Frenchmen and women got a
nasty shock in 1954 after a very bad mistake by a Parisian
pharmacist who had started peddling di-ethyl tim diiodide as a
cure for skin infections. British scientists were in the very same
year working to prove how toxic the chemical was. It had
already been shown (in 1931) to be utterly useless in the
treatment of boils. Nonetheless the French drug-manufacturer
managed to poison 217 French boil-sufferers, 110 of whom
died, before his medicine was banned.

Spruce Goose

American film director and fighter pilot Howard Hughes made being hopelessly out of touch into a life's work by locking himself up in his mansion for years and years and refusing to cut his nails or brush his hair. Perhaps he was trying to make an obscure point about a strange incident from his past.

In the 1940s Hughes had been a national hero in America. He had held the national speed record three times and was one of the first pilots ever to fly the whole way around the world single-handed. He arrived back in New York to be greeted by a ticker tape parade on Broadway.

During the Second World War, pilots on both sides and particularly such daredevil ones as Howard Hughes, were confident that the way to achieve victory was by improving their power in the air. This was a very difficult area to work in, since the bigger the aircraft, the more it disturbs the air around itself, sending out pressure waves which eventually bring the craft crashing to the ground. The problem had appeared to be insoluble.

Spruce Goose

With a friend, the leading industrialist Henry Kaiser, Howard Hughes thought that he would be the first person to crack a problem that had been troubling designers all over the world for decades. Together they went to the US government with the design for a plane which would be the answer to all of the Allies' problems. They had created the drawings for a plane which would also be a giant flying boat and which would therefore be able to supply the troops on D-day with all of the ammunition and so on that they might need. The government was keen. They gave Hughes 18 million dollars to create the world's largest passenger plane and Hughes, who was a perfectionist, started work on what became known technically as the H-4. In order to overcome the air pressure and weight obstacles, the plane was to be built entirely out of wood.

The H-4 was a terrible mistake. It cost far, far more than anyone had ever thought it would. Terrible technical problems could not be overcome. It weighed far too much ever to get off the ground. By the time the design was complete, the Second World War had already finished. Howard Hughes' reputation was ruined. He was determined to make the plane fly. He organised a massive public demonstration for the H-4's maiden flight. The massive object with its wingspan of 320 feet and its 700 passenger capacity caught the imagination of the public, who christened the giant wooden plane the "Spruce Goose". Large numbers turned up to see it soar high into the air with their hero at its wheel.

On 2 November 1947, Howard Hughes flew the Spruce Goose on its one and only flight. It went precisely 70 feet before it came crashing down into the ocean below. Hughes was not hurt physically but conceded that the whole project had been one terrible mistake. He was disgraced and hauled before a Senate Committee to explain why he had thrown away such an enormous sum of money on such an absurd project. He was accused of war profiteering and political pay-offs. Although he was eventually acquitted, Howard Hughes was a ruined man, having lost everything except his gargantuan fortune. The Spruce Goose itself was installed in a specially designed hangar-museum at Long Beach, south of Los Angeles, right alongside the Queen Mary. Howard Hughes' mistake has become one of California's leading tourist attractions.

Love Is Blind

"I don't think there'll be a war. The Fuhrer doesn't want his new buildings bombed" said Fascist bimbo Unity Mitford in 1938. See Chapter 2.

I t may seem a contradiction in terms for a whole nation to be out of touch, but if you read this story about the Americans in 1938 there really is no other conclusion.

War of the Worlds

In 1938 Orson Welles, with two colleagues, created a production company for radio plays called Mercury Theatre. They had a regular slot on Sunday evenings on CBS radio but were handicapped in their grasp for media fame and fortune by the fact that no-one listened to it.

Welles therefore decided to pull out all the stops and go for the big one. He would dramatise a version of H.G. Wells' *The War of the Worlds* and the team would endeavour to make it as realistic as possible. It would all be terrifically dramatic and after five days of rehearsals everyone was rearing to go. Assisted by the fact that there was, for a change, nothing good on the other channel, the War of the Worlds had an unusually high tune-in rating. Straight after the weather report, the show was introduced by a linkman stating:

"Ladies and gentlemen, I have a grave announcement to make. The strange object which fell at Grovers Mill, New Jersey, earlier this evening was not a meteorite. Incredible as it seems, it contained strange beings who are believed to be the vanguard of an army from the planet Mars."

The production continued in what the actors considered to be a highly ear-catching way with no straight narrative but a series of up-to-the-minute bulletins about hideous, scaly creatures from Mars running amok all over the exotic surroundings of New Jersey. Another announcer cut in to urge the people of the world not to panic but, as it happened, thousands of citizens all over America were currently being slaughtered by the deathly force of ray guns. The climax of the play was an announcer apparently screaming that Manhattan had been taken over by aliens and then trailing off into an anguished death rattle and then silence.

The actors were not wrong. Their thespian skills were so convincing that by the time the production ended, thousands of people had already fled their homes and were heading for that traditional haven from landing Martians, the hills. In New Jersey, where panic was at its greatest, whole families packed into their station wagons with wet towels over their heads, since they assumed this would save them from the deadly effects of Martian poison gas.

The only people who were unaware of the national State of Emergency were those inside the CBS studio who all, shattered after a hard day's serious acting, went straight home to bed. Orson Welles awoke the next day to find his name spread like mud over the front pages of all the national newspapers. Dozens of people brought cases for shock against CBS but none of them were pursued. Mercury Theatre would never be "that programme on the other channel" again and Orson Welles, who was only twenty-four at the time, was instantaneously a star.

Welsh Prophet

In 1964 Richard Burton announced "I have the last say in everything with Liz now."

Politics of Sex

Amid the clamour of public outcry at the Profumo affair in 1963 was the single quavering voice of potty Tory MP Reginald

Paget. "What do these rumours amount to?" asked the polite parliamentarian. "They amount to the fact that a minister is said to be acquainted with a very pretty girl. I should have thought that was a matter for congratulation rather than enquiry."

Viewing Figures

It could be judged a mistake on the part of one of the French television channels that they broadcast a programme in 1978 which was watched by a grand total of 0% of the population.

This staggeringly unsuccessful statistic was achieved by a programme which featured a half-hour monologue by an Armenian woman, talking about her life with her husband. This broadcast, which had come highly recommended in the television sections of various daily newspapers, was beaten in the ratings stakes by *It's a Knockout* and a drama about the French Revolution.

Assassination Family

Senator Robert F. Kennedy arrived at Nairobi airport to meet Tom Mboya, a minister of the Kenyan government. He was flattered to find a huge crowd to greet him and smiled cheerily at them, giving them a broad thumbs-up sign. This was greeted with more applause and riotous cheering. Mboya explained to Kennedy later that the single raised thumb was the campaign sign of the Kenyan Communist Party.

Boxing Prophet

"In the future amusements will be intelligent and educational, games of brute strength will die out and there will be new games of mental skill. Boxers, footballers and others who rely mainly upon their strength for a living will be regarded as 'throw-outs' of low mental capacity" A. M. Low, 1925 (but he wasn't entirely wrong).

Celebrity Out-of-Touchers

A BBC interviewer asked John Lennon live on air if he made "conscious use of onomatopoeia". "I dunno what that fellow was on about," said John later. "He kept on talking about an automatic pier."

"The first proposition that the sun is the centre and does not revolve around the earth is foolishly absurd and false and heretical. The second proposition that the earth is not the centre but revolves about the sun is absurd, false in philosophy and, from a theological point of view at least, opposed to truth." Inquisition on Galileo.

"The energy produced by the breaking down of the atom is a very poor kind of thing. Anyone who looks for a source of power in the transformation of the atom is talking moonshine." Sir Ernest Rutherford, originator of nuclear theory and pioneer atom-splitter in 1933.

Dead Cert

In 1936 John Langdon-Davies published a book called *A Short History of the Future* which contained the following predictions:

"Democracy will be dead by 1950"

"There will be no war in Western Europe in the next five years" and

"Crime will be considered a disease after 1985 and will cease to exist by 1990"

That Time of the Month Again

One of London's leading teaching hospitals recently installed a new computer programme in its gynaecology department. This high-tech device would manage time more efficiently, thus saving costs and improving appointment schedules to the benefit of all.

One of its most important improvements was to ask the lady patient automatically if she was currently menstruating in order not to waste the doctor's time before she got into the surgery. If the answer was "yes", the computer would efficiently and effectively give her a new appointment date straight away – for four weeks' time.

Unholy Alliance

"Now let's all try to settle this problem in a true Christian spirit." Senator Warren Austin at the UN on the Arab-Israeli conflict in 1948.

Over My Dead Body

On 22 March 1979 the Indian Prime Minister, Mr Morarji Desai, broke the sad news to Parliament that the nation's elder statesman and respected patriot, Jayaprakash Narayan, had passed away in a Bombay hospital earlier that day.

The whole nation went into mourning. Mr Desai paid a moving tribute to a man that the whole country had loved. Parliament was suspended for the rest of the day whilst flags all over the country were lowered to half-mast and funeral music was broadcast on the national radio station.

Everyone in the country was saddened to hear this mournful music emanating from their radio sets, not least Mr Narayan himself who woke up to the sound of his own demise. The Prime Minister was terribly apologetic but explained to a bemused and living Mr Narayan that he had received the infallible information about his demise from the director of the India's National Intelligence Bureau.

Sum Idiot

''I am still seeking in fact for anything that Einstein has added to mathematical knowledge'' Arthur Lynch, 1932.

- chapter thirteen -

THROWING THE BALL INTO THE AIR BEFORE YOU'VE CAUGHT IT

T his is a small but lovely chapter dedicated to mistake category 13, the "premature celebration". The phrase, for those not familiar with it, is a cricketing one. In order to indicate, when fielding, that you have caught out one of the batsmen, you throw the ball into the air. Some players in the field of life are so excited by this prospect that they throw the ball as high as they are able, before they have actually grasped it firmly in their hands, thus rendering the catch null and void.

Throwing the Skull into the Court Before You Know How Old It Is

Peter Reyn-Bart of Knightsbridge was being questioned about the mysterious disappearance twenty-three years earlier of his lovely wife, Marika. He denied emphatically that she was even dead, stating that he had always been devastated by her desertion and return to the Lebanon.

The police went to his old house near Wilmslow in Cheshire where they discovered a skull in a peat bog by his garden. Confronted with the news Reyn-Bart collapsed and immediately confessed to having strangled his wife and then chopped her to pieces and buried her remains. He was jailed for life.

The skull that the police had found dated from the year 410 AD. There had been no other evidence to link Reyn-Bart to the crime.

Throwing the Car onto the Road Before You've Built It

There is little doubt that in the land of techno-bollocks the car-maker is king.

Aston Martin Lagonda

The 1976 London Motor Show was dominated by the arrival of a new Aston Martin Lagonda which cost more than £32,000 and was claimed to go at a rate of 140 miles per hour.

The very first model was bought by the Marchioness of Tavistock as a seventeenth wedding anniversary present for her beloved husband, the Duke of Bedford. The handing over ceremony was publicised in a very grand way and large numbers of journalists turned up to witness the super-event in the splendid surroundings of the ancestral home, Woburn Abbey. Three months earlier, the mini-computer which was due to revolutionise motor mechanics had blown up. It had never quite recovered. As four embarrassed technicians pushed the Lagonda down the magnificent driveway at Woburn, the world's newest deluxe sports car managed a grand total of 1 mile per hour.

Throwing the Confetti in the Air Before You've Partied

Peter Sellers once went to a party in the country at which he danced all night with a very beautiful stranger. He was quite captivated by her charming looks and personality and determined to accompany her home. They left the party together and Peter thought his luck was in. There was a full moon and the evening was warm. Perhaps, suggested Mr Sellers tentatively, he might be allowed to accompany his lovely companion along the bridle path?

"Oh no, I'm terribly sorry," was her immediate and frank response, "it's far too early to be thinking about marriage."

. chapter fourteen .

OLD BALONEY

*T*he word baloney is a corruption of Bologna, a town in Italy famous for sausages. If people wanted to say that something was nonsense (ie it fitted into mistake category 14) they would say "It's a load of old Italian sausages" or just "old baloney".

Barbara Cartland's Hot Advice For Lovers

Just a quick word of advice from that wellpool of sexual know-how – Barbara Cartland.

"White sugar," she tells us, "causes fatigue and sexual apathy between husband and wife. My recipe against sexual fatigue is to take honey in large quantities, two Gev-E-Tabs, ten vitamin E pills, four wheatgerm oil tablets, four vitamin A pills, four bonemeal tablets, six liver-plus tablets and two dessert spoons of Bio-Strath Elixir, twice a day."

So now you know.

Toad in the Baloney

It used to be a very commonly held misconception that toads secrete a deadly venom. The husband of an Italian woman was dying of dropsy, but taking far too long over the business for her liking. She accordingly procured a toad and put it into his wine so that he might drink the liquid and die. Instead, and much to her astonishment, he completely recovered overnight.

As everyone knows, toad venom is the single best cure for dropsy.

Masturbation and Orgasms

A gentleman named Orson Squire Fowler wrote a book in 1870 called *Sexual Science* which is just jam-packed with technical advice, almost all of which is wrong. He does revel particularly in an entire chapter devoted to advice for the families of the sufferers of that appalling sickness, masturbation:

> Victims of self-abuse have pallid, bloodless counte-
> nances, hollow, sunken and half-ghastly eyes, with a
> red rim around the eyelids and black and blue semi-
> circles around the eyes. Red pimples on the face with
> a black spot in their middles are a sure sign of self-
> pollution in males, and irregularities in females.
> Stance is another sign. Self-polluters often stand
> and sit in the posture assumed during masturbation
> (*what might that be, we wonder?*). They also often carry
> their hands to the private parts, and in laughing they
> throw this part of their bodies forward.
>
> Masturbation poisons your body, breaks down
> your nerves, paralyses your whole system. When
> practised before puberty, it dwarfs and enfeebles
> the sexual organs . . . hundreds have been brought
> to our lunatic asylums by this single form of vice,
> and some must be tied down to prevent further
> destruction.

The special masturbation mistake award, however, must go to Rudolf Friedman, a psychiatrist in the 1950s, who wrote that the biggest single give-away was "the long, thin, almost imperceptible black hair growing out of the middle of the palm of the left hand of masturbators." We've all noticed a number of people suffering from that complaint. They all, no doubt, eat cornflakes for breakfast, which, as every student of the area knows, were invented as a remedy for this very ailment. A bowl a day keeps the black hair away.

Lord Kelvin

"X-rays will prove to be a hoax" Lord Kelvin, President of the Royal Society, 1890-95.

F or more baloney from Lord Kelvin, see Chapter 12, 'Hopelessly out of Touch'.

No Spies on Me

On 5 May 1960 Dwight Eisenhower categorically denied that there was any US spying programme over the Soviet Union after Kruschev had claimed that a U2 had been shot down. Eisenhower had to eat his words later that day when the pilot of the U2 appeared on the Soviet TV News.

Oh No He Didn't

The actual line in the Warner Bros. World War II film *Casablanca*, is not "Play it Again, Sam" at all. It is not even

Humphrey Bogart who utters the words. In fact it is Ingrid Bergman who says to the piano-playing Dooley Wilson "Play it, Sam. Play *As Time Goes By*."

In any event, Sam doesn't play, he merely sings, since Dooley Wilson couldn't actually play the piano, the sound of which was dubbed in at a later date.

Hoisted by Your Own Petard

It is a common mistake to think that this expression has anything to do with hoisting or hanging or ropes. See Chapter 6.

Smoked Out

In 1869 the editor of a scientific journal called *English Mechanic* published what he considered to be the definitive answer to a letter from an elderly smoker asking for advice as to how best to give up nicotine:

> The best and only antidote I know for the effects of tobacco on the nervous system is tincture of ferric chloride, or generally known by druggists as tinct. ferri sesquicholoride, from 10 to 20 minims (two drops are about one minim of a tincture) in a glass of sherry – or in water if alcoholic liquor is objected to – taken immediately after smoking, or other excessive use of tobacco, is a complete restorative. If you were to take this two or three times a day your shakiness would probably much diminish; but let me give you one piece of advice, not to give up smoking, as at your age it would do no good.

Baldies In

A Victorian doctor, called W.G. Black, became very anxious about a marked increase in baldness amongst the young doctors of his day. He published a long treatise on the subject, none of which has any scientific basis, and the highlights of which are probably:

> This decay of hair so early in the youth and manhood of the present day may be due to the fashion of short cropping of the head, even in boys now, as there is little or no baldness noticed in women, who are not cropped short in their hair, not even as girls.
>
> The explanation of this decay, which seems to be irremediable in maturing age, is probably due to the young hairs budding out at the side of the older growth being deprived of shelter and warmth to keep up their young vitality and they consequently wither down from exposure. The stronger hair only can therefore survive this exposure to the weather and it even is being stunted in growth owing to its being frequently cropped short. A like process goes on in meadow and cornfields when the coarser stubble and straw and grass would allow the growth amongst them of fine grass, weeds and flowers which would perish if left alone without any shelter.

This is no less potty, however, than the current belief, common amongst 90s baldies, that you can prevent baldness by shaving your head. You might as well try and prevent athlete's foot by cutting off your leg.

In Di Balls

The nineteenth-century German, Dr Sixt, developed a tremendous but mistaken theory called the Testicle Theory to explain the respective conception of male and female babies. Sixt decided that in any given intercourse the man ejaculated from one testicle only. The right testicle produced boys and the left produced girls. Sixt gives careful instructions to couples hoping to conceive sons. The husband was supposed to lie to the right of his wife and to board his wife by raising the right knee, leaving the right testicle as high as possible on the belly of the lady. "If the left testicle should somehow become drawn up towards the abdomen," says Sixt, "it may be pushed down quite easily during coition and the right one pushed up to be sure of attaining the desired end. Try it and let me know how you get on."

The last word on the area, however, has to be that of the Greek philosopher, Aristotle, who felt he had the whole problem covered:

"Erection is chiefly caused by scuraum, eringoes, cresses, crysmon, parsnips, artichokes, turnips, asparagus, candied ginger, acorns bruised to powder and drankin muscadel, scallion and, finally, sea shell fish."

Old Maids' Tales

Woman's Own – 14 January 1944

Dear Agony Aunt
We are two not so young women who have lost our fiancés in the war. We shall never have any other lovers, because the past was so perfect. But is it true that unmarried women get peculiar and suffer in health?

Dear ladies
Anyone may get peculiar but there is no need for it. What makes some unmarried women difficult and peculiar is that they have found no channel for their emotions and become embittered or eccentric. You can find such a channel in work you like; in love for people or animals or in study of various sorts;

anything living or creative will keep you just as pleasant as if you had married. I sympathise so deeply in your loss.

Home Notes – 24 November 1928

Doris – is it possible for a man to fall in love with a girl who has false teeth?

Answer: Of course it is. It happens every day.

• chapter fifteen •

BARKING MAD

In 1958 the West Midlands Police Force thought that they had come up with the ultimate solution for traffic control – a helmet with a flashing blue lamp on top.

The helmet, fitted with a battery-powered light, was top heavy and kept falling off every time PC Jim Sparks – the lucky constable selected for the test run – tried to turn his head to watch the oncoming cars.

"A right Charlie I felt, too," he said. "People were staring at me open-mouthed as they drove past. I'd never been so embarrassed. It was before fluorescent clothing and it could be downright dangerous on traffic duty – you had to be pretty nimble on your feet – but the flashing helmet wasn't any use. The chin strap dug into me and, because it was so heavy with the batteries in the top of the helmet, it was just about impossible to control. Every time I moved my head, the helmet simply fell off."

After PX Sparks had fought valiantly with the helmet for over an hour and a half, senior officers conceded that the idea might be a mistake. The prototype headgear disappeared into the mists of time until Mr Sparks, now retired, responded to a call from West Midlands Police Museum in Birmingham for memorabilia. "When they saw the photograph," he said, "they couldn't believe it and they all fell about laughing."

C ategory 15 mistakes cannot be attributed to anything except the fact that their perpetrators have a kangaroo loose in the top paddock.

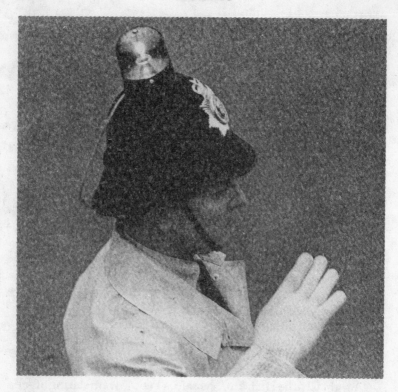

This is a picture of a policeman with a light on his head

Lunatic General

The appointment of Sir William Erskine as a senior commander during the Peninsular War was a mistake to rival the very best. The Duke of Wellington was astonished at the commission and wrote immediately to the Military Secretary in London to complain that Erskine was well-known to be barking mad. "No doubt he is a little mad at times," replied the Secretary by post, "but in his lucid intervals he is a jolly nice chap . . . though I must say that he did look a little mad as he embarked." Erskine's record wasn't too impressive either. His astonishingly bad eye-sight had made him a complete liability at the battle of Sabugal in 1811, where he had led a charge *away from the enemy* by mistake.

At the battle of Almeida, all of Wellington's forebodings were fulfilled. The Iron Duke was closing in on the besieged French garrison and victory seemed assured. Aware of the dangers of placing too much on the madman's shoulders, Wellington asked him to perform the simple task of guarding the bridge of Barba de Puerca. There were no charges to be made and no pitfalls into which Erskine's loopiness or his short-sightedness could lead him. He just had to stand there with a mixed battalion of cavalry and infantry and stop the French getting out.

Erskine was having dinner when Wellington's order arrived. His first response (madder than even Wellington could have anticipated), was to send a corporal and four men to guard the bridge. One of the other dinner guests was so shocked by this stupidity that he blurted out "Sir William, you might as well attempt to block up the bridge with a pinch of snuff."

This brought on one of Erskine's famous moments of lucidity. He immediately wrote out an order to send a whole regiment to block the bridge. "Better safe than sorry" he added.

Unfortunately, this moment of lucidity was a particularly brief one. As soon as he had finished writing out the order, Erskine folded it up, put it in his pocket and forgot about it. When the French realised the danger of their position and decided to retreat, they were amazed to find the bridge unguarded and escaped without a single casualty. Wellington called it "the most disgraceful military event that has yet occurred to us."

When Erskine subsequently committed suicide by jumping out of a window in Lisbon in 1813, his last words were "Why on earth did I do that?"

Plain Cuckoo

"One of Colorado's oldest citizens and a resident of Walsenburg for about a century died here yesterday. Mrs Quintina was

104 years old at the time of her death, her grandmother said."
Enterprise Times, Brockton, Massachusetts

Ronald the Toast-Maker

In 1982 Ronald Reagan was in Brazil at a political function and, towards the end of the meal, he was asked to make a speech.

"Now would you join me in a toast to President Figueiredo," he said, "and to all the people of Bolivia . . . oh no, that's wrong, that's where I'm going next . . . erm . . . to the people of Brazil, yes that's right, Brazil." His voice trailed off as one of his aides drew his attention to the fact that his next destination was in fact Bogota, the capital of Colombia.

Mad Jimmy Carter

"A great man who should have been President and would have been one of the greatest Presidents in history – Hubert Horatio Hornblower." Jimmy Carter at the 1980 Democratic Convention on Hubert Humphrey.

Cereal Killer

Pat Coombs, a comedienne of the 1970s, holds the record for the highest number of mistakes in one shoot on a television commercial. In 1973 she astonished her camera crew by forgetting the name of the product she was supposed to be advertising on a record-breaking twenty-eight takes. This truly stupendous feat of memory is still with her since, on being questioned about the advertisement five years after the event, she was still unable to remember anything beyond the fact that it was a kind of Swiss breakfast cereal.

Shortly afterwards the product was withdrawn. Ms Coombs no longer eats muesli.

Fighting for Survival

In May 1981 two old men, who had been living opposite each other in Cleveland, Ohio for fifty years, had finally had enough.

The men, one aged seventy-seven and one aged seventy-six, began quarrelling in their mutual hallway at about 11 am on Tuesday. Neither would give way and so they both went back into their apartments and came out with antique pistols. They were standing just five feet apart during the duel and fired six shots each. All twelve bullets went astray. Police theorised that they missed because one needed a cane to prop himself up whilst firing, and the other had trouble with his vision since he suffered from acute glaucoma.

Residents called the police, who took the pair to the local station for interview. "There were bullet holes above, bullet holes below and bullet holes all over the hallway," said one of the detectives, "but none anywhere about the person of either of the old folk."

The men were released after both signed papers saying that they did not wish to press charges against the other. Police kept the guns which may go into the local museum.

Kinky Devils

During the seventies the telekinetic powers of Uri Geller, who was best known for his ability to bend metal objects by merely looking at them, were much in vogue. So much so that a young lady in Sweden took out court proceedings against him for causing her unwanted pregnancy. She claimed that as a result of the fact that she and her boyfriend had been watching him on the television whilst making love on the sofa her IUD had been warped and rendered useless.

Pill Talk

The politician, Sir Alan Sterling Parks, declared in 1970 that "no woman should be kept on the pill for 20 years until, in fact, a sufficient number have been kept on the pill for 20 years."

Loch Ness Monster

The dominating geographical feature of the Scottish Highlands is, of course, the Great Glen, a rift valley sixty miles long which splits the country in two and contains, on its bed, three of Scotland's most famous Lochs – Lochy, Oich and Ness. Of these Loch Ness is undoubtedly the most famous and the most spectacular. Eight rivers feed into it and it is deeper than the North Sea and most of the Atlantic Ocean. It has never been known to freeze. It is very, very long and very, very narrow and its steep wooded banks form a wind-funnel giving rise, at times, to immensely beautiful but tidal-like waves.

It is most likely these physical properties that gave rise to the legend of the Loch Ness Monster – or Nessiteras Rhombopteryx, as Sir Peter Scott dubbed the doughty dino' in the mad mid-eighties. The dotty knight was responsible for a huge amount of serious interest in the "old lady of the lake" until a clever TV pundit noticed that Nessiteras Rhombopteryx was an anagram of "Monster Hoax By Sir Peter S".

Mistaken sightings of Nessie are legion. The first known

report was in the sixth century. St Adamnan, who was a very spiritual man and not known for a propensity to tell lies, reports, in his biography of St Columba, that he saw her as he sailed up the Loch on his way to convert the town of Inverness. Nessie, he said, began to cause rough surfaces and the sailing boat rocked violently as the sailors' stomachs churned and the faces turned green with both fear and nausea. St Columba stood up in the boat and as Nessie's head rose from the surface to face one of the monks in a head-on confrontation Columba spoke soothing words and calmed the fearsome beast who sank slowly and calmly back into the icy depths.

A sixteenth-century chronicle describes "a terrible beast issuing out of the water early one morning about midsummer, knocking down trees and killing three men with its tail". But sightings were sporadic until the twentieth-century when they began to proliferate like crazy, which perhaps has something to do with Nessie's profound effect on local business. An organist from Westminster Cathedral swore he saw her in 1973, and in 1961 as many as thirty guests at a local hotel saw two humps appear in a sudden explosion of surf and swim along the surface of the Loch for fifteen minutes before sinking. A circus owner called Bertram Mills offered £20,000 reward to anyone who could capture the monster for his circus but no-one ever did. Possibly the least successful attempt to do so was that of four firemen from Hemel Hempstead in 1975 who decided that where all of the other hunters had gone wrong was on the gender of Nessie, who must, being a monster, naturally be a man.

They built a thirty-foot long papier maché lady monster to attract their Mr Ness and completed it with false eyelashes, full make-up and a pre-recorded mating call. Possibly their first mistake was that the pre-recorded sound turned out to be that of a male walrus and thus unlikely to attract a conservative monster from the deep; secondly, their outboard motor developed a fault, the boat went into a spin and the paper monster's behind was instantaneously flattened by an unfortunately placed jetty, which could hardly have made her the irresistible object they had hoped for.

Loony Bike

In 1897 Thomas Bennet of 69 High Holborn announced a splendid new design of bicycle.

The front wheel and handlebars looked pretty much the same as they do on a modern bike. The pedals, however, were mounted on a single huge cog communicating directly with a tiny cog at the centre of the back wheel.

The back wheel was very unusual. It was heavy and spoked and had sixteen free-spinning tiny wheels mounted around the edge. The crucial element to Adam's design was that the driver should sit directly on top of this curious wheel. As the pedals went round forwards, the central back wheel would rotate backwards and the tiny wheels around the edge would sort of squidge the cycle forwards. As Adams explained it:

'The weight of the rider is perpendicular to the centre of the small wheel which is under him. Immediately the toothed wheel is turned ever so little by the larger toothed wheel from the crank, the weight of the rider is lifted off the centre of the small wheel under him. This, coupled with the power put forth by the rider on to the pedal, causes the smaller wheel under him to, as it were, slip from under him with tremendous velocity (the heavier the rider the greater the velocity) on to the next small wheel.''

The principle of the thing, thought Adams, was the same as that by which a roller-skater fell over: "when the hind wheels of the skate slip forward from under him, his weight goes off the centre and he loses his equilibrium and goes on to the back of his head with great force (the heavier the man, the heavier he falls).''

"If the skater could have only kept his equilibrium," explains Adams, "he would have gone forward as fast as his skate travelled, instead of being left behind on the floor." By this process, the mad inventor thought that his bicycle could travel at sixty miles per hour.

The number of mistakes involved in this design is frighteningly high. Adams ignores every law of motion in constructing his potty bike. As the modern scientist Alan Sutton points out in his book *A Victorian World of Science* (Iowa, 1986), any rider pedalling Adams bike would remain stock still. The ludicrous back wheel would simply whizz round, with all the little wheels spinning in the opposite direction as they hit the ground or the rider's bottom, which would be horribly bruised by the whole performance.

Green Fingers, No Eyes

Thomas Nuttall (1786-1859) was a scientist with spectacularly little sense of direction. He was, by training, a botanist and went travelling on unsuccessful expeditions all over north-west America. During one trip in 1812, his fellow scientists had to light beacons every evening in order to guide him back to their encampment.

On one sad occasion when he got completely lost, a search party was sent out to retrieve him. Nuttall saw the team coming towards him through the darkness and, rather neurotically, assumed that they were Indians out to capture him. He therefore fled and was finally tracked down three days later when he, quite by accident, wandered straight back into the camp. His most pathetic mistake, however, must be the occasion on which he got so lost that he simply collapsed and went to sleep. A passing Indian came across him and, instead of scalping him, considered him so utterly useless that he carried him three miles up the river and took him back to the camp.